How To Do Your Own
ACCOUNTING
For A Small Business

Robert R. Milliron

First Printing, July 1980
Second Printing, (Revised) June 1982
Third Printing, (Revised) August 1984
Fourth Printing, (Revised) May 1988

ISBN: O-913864-34-X
Library of Congress Catalog Card No. 79-53800

Published by: Enterprise Publishing, Inc.,725 Market Street,Wilmington, DE 19801
1-800-533-2665

This book is sold with the understanding that neither the author nor the publisher
is engaged in rendering legal/financial advice. If professional advice is required, the
service of an attorney or accountant should be sought.
Publisher cannot in any way guarantee forms in this book are being used for
the purpose intended and therefore, assumes no responsibility for their proper
and correct use.

*This Enterprise publication is available at a special discount when ordered in large
quantities. Contact: Enterprise Publishing, Inc., Trade Sales Department,
725 N. Market Street, Wilmington, DE 19801, or call 1-800-533-2665 for information.*

Printed in the United States of America.

Acknowledgements

I want to extend my thanks to Thomas Butler, CPA, for taking time from a busy schedule to review my book.

I also desire to acknowledge the help given me by the Internal Revenue Service employees in obtaining the necessary forms to complete the book.

My appreciation goes to Beverly Horning Natrin, editor of Enterprise Publishing, Inc., for the patience and consideration given me during the writing of the additional material. It was a bright light in what I thought was going to be a dark endeavor.

And I want to acknowledge my wife, Helen, who said she knew I could do it all along.

—*Robert R. Milliron*

Our thanks to Boorum & Pease Co. of Elizabeth, New Jersey, for kindly allowing us to reproduce their accounting forms in this book.

—*The Editor.*

*I dedicate this book to
my wife, Helen, who compelled me to face up
to the challenge, and to the many small shop
owners who showed me that
such a book would be valuable.*

Table of Contents

3: The Beginning of a Double-Entry Cash Method of Accounting for Tax Purposes

4: Your Accounting System

5: Posting to the General Ledger from the Cash and Sales Journal

6: Posting to the General Ledger from the Double-Entry Check Register

7: Posting to the General Ledger from the General Journal

8: The State Quarterly Tax and Federal Tax Forms

9: Accounting for the Expanding Business

10: A Simple Costing System for the Small Business

11: The More Sophisticated Forms of Accounting

12: Business Entities and What They Mean to You

Appendix

Introduction

Every year, more than 400,000 new businesses are started in the United States. Less than twenty percent of them survive beyond the third year of existence. These new businesses are often started by people who have a dream and high hopes, but absolutely no knowledge of bookkeeping or its value to the business. Without an adequate bookkeeping system, the business is doomed to failure from the beginning.

This book was written to help the very small business proprietor in overcoming this handicap.

Robert R. Milliron

1

In the Beginning...

"What kind of bookkeeping system should I have for my business?"

In setting up an accounting system for a small business, there are two factors which the person who is doing the bookkeeping must consider. Both of these factors will have a strong bearing on the manner in which the accounting is to be performed, and how accurate the income statements will be when they are prepared from the information available.

Different Types of Accounting

There are two systems of accounting as designated by the Internal Revenue Service for accounting-for-taxes. The first is the *cash basis* and the second is the *accrual basis.* Of the two, the cash basis is the simplest. However, because of the nature of some businesses, there are types of small enterprises which cannot use the cash basis of accounting.

In the cash basis of reporting income, all monies are not counted as being earned until they are actually paid into the cash box or register. This type of business is often called a "cash and carry" and covers such ventures as the drive-up vegetable stand, the barber shop, the beauty parlor, the shoe repair shop, and so forth. Naturally, some of these types of businesses could also operate on a credit basis. Here they would need to maintain some record of the credit transactions in order to know how much money they would have coming in and from where. This is really the beginning of an accrual system, and will be dealt with in the corresponding section of this book.

So in the cash basis of accounting, the money is not entered into the books until it is actually received. Then it is entered into that day's business, regardless of when the merchandise may have been purchased by the customer.

Cash and Credit

I will run through this again in another way.

In accounting on the cash basis, monies received for merchandise sold are not entered into the books until actually received regardless of when the merchandise might have been sold to the customer. Joe Wilson buys vegetables at the local stand, then tells the farmer that he is short of funds and will pay him on Friday. The money will be entered into the farmer's books on Friday when the farmer received the money, NOT when the vegetables are actually sold to Joe. However, this is still a cash basis of accounting the transaction, in spite of the fact that Joe "charged" vegetables for a few days.

In order that the small business owner will understand the cash basis method of bookkeeping and accounting for tax purposes and the make-up of Income Statements, I want to emphasize that the same manner used in the handling of cash received must also be used in recording payment for merchandise purchased from the distributor for resale. Often, such purchases may be paid with cash on the spot when doing business with a supply store, farmer, or parts house, depending on the kind of business involved. If the business is large enough and buys enough merchandise from its vendors, the owner may have merchandise on hand for sale that has been invoiced but will not be paid for until sometime the following month.

This is classified as buying on "open account" and is a charge business for the vending company. When the small business owner pays for this merchandise (usually around the tenth of the following month), the owner will still enter the transaction in the cash method records. This is done by posting it from the check stub in the business week or month in which the check was written. This type of transaction will be expained more in detail later in the book.

Right now, I want only to explain the two methods of accounting which are used in business. In the cash method section, I will explain in detail how to work with the unpaid invoices at the end of the month so that you will have an accurate income statement, and will know how much profit you are actually clearing from your business.

Inaccurate bookkeeping will give an inaccurate profit or loss statement, and you could end up paying taxes on money which was never earned.

The Accrual Method of Accounting for Tax Purposes

In doing business on the accrual bookkeeping or accounting basis, the firm which does a large amount of credit business, or sells a great quantity to their customers on a credit basis, finds that a larger amount of bookkeeping is necessary to record all the transactions involved. In using the accrual method, the business owner counts all business as sales at the time they are made, regardless of whether the sale is a cash transaction (paid for at the time of the sale) or a charge (to be paid for at some later date). In doing so, the amount of the charge business is added to the cash sales figure. The combination of the two are the total sales for the given time.

The same method is also used in accounting for the cost of merchandise purchased for resale, including merchandise purchased on open account and for which payment has not been made. Open account buying by the owner often brings large amounts of merchandise into the store that are invoiced but not paid for. Much of it could even be sold to the owner's customers before payment is made to the vendor.

If the invoices for this merchandise were not recorded in some manner, the sales for the month (less the cost of the merchandise sold) would leave a profit figure which would be erroneous. This profit would be larger because all of the cost of the merchandise sold would not have been recorded.

In order to have an accurate system under these circumstances, all invoices are usually posted to an invoice register so that the totals can be posted to a "general ledger." They are then added into costs before the income statement is drawn.

What "Accrual" Means

This is the purpose of the accrual method of accounting. The owner is *accruing* costs not yet paid, or adding them in, so that the net profit picture will be most accurate. This will be explained in more detail in the double entry accounting section of the book.

To clarify the two methods of accounting for taxes, I will repeat the very basics of each method.

The Cash Method: Income, or money due for merchandise sold or services rendered, is not counted as earned until it is actually received, regardless of when the sale was made or service was rendered.

The cost or payment for the merchandise sold, as invoiced by the wholesale house, is not recorded or entered as an expense until the time it is actually paid.

The Accrual Method: The accrual method of accounting is to post or enter in the books all sales whether the money was received at the time of the sale or not. Usually posted from a sales slip or from cash register tapes (receipts) at the end of the day of business.

Cost of the merchandise sold is recorded as soon as the invoice is received from the vendor and entered into books as cost of sales or inventory purchase. This gives the shopkeeper an accurate record of what purchases are and what inventory is on hand, on a daily basis.

Now that you know what the two systems or methods involve, and have some knowledge of what it's all about, I ask that you forget about them for now.

We will be looking at the cash method first. This is a simple method for the small business, and it is almost foolproof. In using it and enlarging upon it as your business grows, you will gradually work into a double entry accounting system which will give you all of the information you need to control your business.

If you turn your business into a corporation, you might eventually be required to use the accrual method of accounting. The accrual method is required for tax purposes for regular corporations and for partnerships with corporations as partners. A small corporation is not required to use the cash method as long as the average gross receipts for the prior three years does not exceed $5 million. When the business has not been in existence for three years, you use the average annual gross receipts for whatever period the business has been in existence. This means that it probably will be a while before you are required to use the accrual method, but it is a point to keep in mind.

2

The Simple Way To Go

Needed: A columnar pad and a sharp pencil.

Suggested: ● Improvised check records and sales records made from Boorum & Pease No. 8910 10-column pad.

● Improvised Compensation sheet made from Burroughs H556 columnar pad.

● Improvised Flatform ledger made from Boorum & Pease No. 4825, 25-column pad.

These or similar pads should be available at your office supply store.

The Cash Method of Accounting for Taxes

When Paulus the aristocrat opened the gates of his courtyard along the Appian Way in ancient Rome and permitted a lone tradesman to set up shop, he created the need for a form of endeavor which is the most misunderstood profession on earth. In giving space in return for part of the profits, it became necessary for the tradesman to keep a record of his transactions. This was because he needed to know how much of his income had to be passed along to his landlord. It has been a very necessary part of the business world ever since.

Since those first early sales of olive oil and sweet herbs, there have been other expense additions made to the system of accounting. But the general theory remains exactly the same. Each amount of money that comes from sales is counted. From it is deducted the cost of operating the business, so that a net profit is determined. It is on the net profit that a business pays taxes that go to the government. Government requires that an adequate bookkeeping system be maintained in order to fulfill this obligation.

The Sale

So, in the beginning, we have a sale. From that sale the tradesman deducted the cost of the item he had sold. He then divided the balance between himself and Paulus the aristocrat. However, in the passing months, the tradesman discovered that in order to carry on the business, he often had to leave it for long periods of time. This meant replacing himself with someone who could carry on his business and see that all of his expenses were paid. So it was that the first bookkeeper came into being.

Romulus, a genteel slave, became the operator of the store. He prepared records so that his master would know how much money came into the store and to whom it belonged. Throughout the passing years, the business grew from a small oil and herb shop into something much larger. The business eventually sold meat and salt and perfumes for the women, and beautiful linens for the ladies of Paulus and his friends.

Paulus was a very benevolent landlord and accepted a smaller percentage of the profits on certain types of merchandise and, in rare instances, no percentage at all. Because of this, it was necessary for Romulus to keep the various kinds of merchandise sales separated so that the amounts of the various items could be known.

Previously, the tradesman had found his sales a very simple thing. A customer came into the shop, made a purchase, paid for it, and carried it home with him. The money received for that sale belonged to the tradesman who thrust it into his pocket and waited for his next customer.

The Cash Drawer

Romulus found his sales more difficult. Because the money he received was not his own, he couldn't put it into his pocket. He found it necessary to keep it in a box, or some other place of safekeeping, until he could turn it over to his master. In order to prove to his master that the money in the box was the actual amount taken in on sales, he had to write down the amount of each sale so he could add them up and compare the amount with the sum turned over to his master.

At that time in bookkeeping history, the entry on his record pad was very simple. Romulus simply wrote down the amount of the sale and the kind of merchandise sold.

Olive Oil	$ 1.97
Perfume	2.36
Dagger Tip	7.95
Leather Shield	14.95
Total Sale	$27.23

(Naturally the early Roman values were not in dollars and cents, and the sales might not have been daggers and shields, but the operations were the same.) The total of the products sold, when added, amounted to $27.23, and the amount of money in the cash box should have added up to that amount. When it did, the tradesman was probably very pleased and undoubtedly gave Romulus a gentle pat on the back.

Whenever the tradesman was gone for long periods of time, Romulus found that a large amount of merchandise had been ordered by his master and was delivered to the shop. It was left to him to pay for this merchandise out of the store's funds. In order to keep track of these payments, he found it necessary to set up a merchandise purchase-and-expense sheet so that he would be able to show his master where the money was going. Feed vendors delivered hay for his master's horses, and this had to be posted as an expense of the store. His master used the horses to pull his chariot on his buying trips. Bolts of cloth, additional vials of perfume, kegs of olive oil, and weapons were delivered to the store. Romulus had to pay for all of these items.

As he paid for each delivery, he entered the amount of the purchase on his merchandise purchase-and-expense sheet. At the end of the day, he tallied it in the same manner as he had done with the cash-received sheet.

One of his sheets might have looked like this:

Paid Out for Merchandise:

23 daggers @ $3.59	=	$ 82.57
4 vials of perfume @ 1.85	=	7.40
6 bolts of fine cloth @ 8.76	=	52.56
3 leather shields @ 7.65	=	22.95
Total Paid Out for Merchandise		$165.48

In determining how much money should be left in his deposit (cash box), it was a simple matter of deducting the paid out amount of $165.48 from his total sales of that day. The balance should be the amount of money left in his box. When this proved to be true, Romulus was very pleased.

A Single Entry Cash Method Bookkeeping System That Works

In time, the tradesman found it necessary to travel far afield in order to obtain merchandise. Romulus was left to tend his shop for days or weeks at a time. The slave found it necessary to keep a larger and more permanent record of his sales and of the payments he made for the merchandise in the store. He did this by making up a form consisting of a number of columns on which he could post the sales at the end of the day. He would then add them all up, yielding a total of his sales for the entire week. This way, he was always ready to show his master how many sales had been made and how much money was held in his small box in the back room.

On his form, he posted all of his sales in columns on the same line and dated each line for the day of the sales. This type of form has carried through to the present time, and we will set up our sales and expense journals in the same manner.

There are a number of columnar pads on the market which are suitable for our work sheets. You can have your choice. Be certain that the general shape is similar to the ones included in the pages of this book. I can recommend the Boorum & Pease Standard pads which can be purchased at any stationery or office supply store. The numbers of the pads I am using are the 8910 10-column pad in green, or the 4910 10-column pad in buff. These pads have ten columns, a description space, and a space for the date. This should be ample for the small bookkeeping system we will work with first.

Figures 1. and 2. are samples of Romulus' pages with account-named columns which were necessary for his sales, purchase and expense items. Let's take a look at them and see what the very simplest form of bookkeeping can be. If you are wondering what this slave bit is all about, bear with me. It has a very important part in explaining why certain business procedures are handled in the manner in which they are today.

The Sales Sheet

For the week illustrated, the shop had sales of olive oil in the amount of $31.37, perfume $6.76, cloth $65.60, weapons $73.10, and miscellaneous (or other) sales of $10.05. Added across from right to left, the total of all the sales equals $186.88, the total of the money in the box or deposit column.

Purchase And Expense Sheet

On this expense sheet, Romulus has posted merchandise costs of $95.90, rent $19.32, hay for horses $7.65, trumpeter to call attention to the shop (advertising) $3.75, oil for the shop lamp $1.65, and water for cleaning and drinking $4.75. Added up across the columns, this comes to a total of $133.02 for his expenses for the week.

Income Statement

In making up a simple income statement, we will first post the amount of sales on a new sheet of paper. This figure was $186.88. Under this, we will post the cost of merchandise sold, which was $95.90. Deduct this figure from the total sales figure, and we have a gross profit of $90.98. Now, because there were expense items paid for out of store funds, we must also post them on our sheet and we will do that item-by-item. Rent was $19.32, hay $7.65, trumpeter $3.75, oil for the lamp $1.65, and water for the shop $4.75. We will post these, one under the other, under a heading of "Operating Expenses."

The result, after adding up the operating expenses and deducting the total from the gross profit, leaves a net profit of $53.86.

If all of the merchandise had been sold and there were no articles left in the store for sale (inventory) this is an accurate income statement and would serve to make out a tax return for the earnings involved. But, remember, *it is not a financial statement.* This is only an income statement, which provides some of the information which is needed to make up a financial statement.

Bartelli the Tradesman
Courtyard of Paulus the Aristocrat
Week June 5 through 12th

Income From Operations

Olive oil	$ 31.37	
Perfume	6.76	
Bolts of cloth	65.60	
Weapons	73.10	
Miscellaneous sales	10.05	
Total Sales		$186.88

Cost of Sales—

Merchandise Purchased		95.90
Gross Profit from Sales		$ 90.98

Operating Expenses

Rent to Paulus	$ 19.32	
Hay for horses	7.65	
Trumpeter to call bargains	3.75	
Oil for shop lamps	1.65	
Water for shop	4.75	
Total cost of operating shop		$ 37.12
Net profit from operations		$ 53.86

Inventory

In working up our bookkeeping system for Romulus, we have assumed that he carried very little or no inventory on hand, and the amount of his merchandise purchased was also the amount of merchandise sold (in terms of items, not monetary value). However, at this stage of our system, let us assume that Romulus did have a beginning inventory. By actual physical count at the beginning statement period, this consisted of two vials of perfume at $1.85 each, one leather shield at $7.65, and one bolt of cloth at $8.76. This would give him an inventory value of $20.11.

To this amount, we will add his merchandise purchases of $95.90, which would give him a total of $116.01 in merchandise available for sale to his customers.

Now suppose that after the sales period, Romulus counted his merchandise again and discovered that he had remaining one vial of perfume at $1.85 and one leather shield at $7.65, or a total of $9.50. In order to discover the cost of the merchandise he had sold, he must deduct the $9.50 from the total of the beginning inventory, and add the purchases of $116.01. Subtract $9.50 from $116.01 leaving a balance of $106.51, which is the new cost of the merchandise which was drawn from the total inventory in the form of sales.

Figure 1

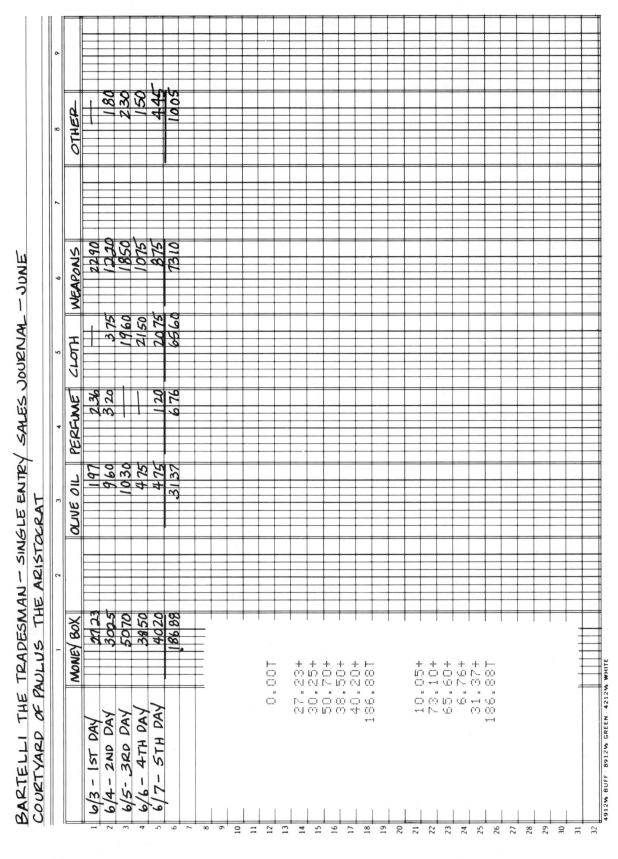

Figure 2

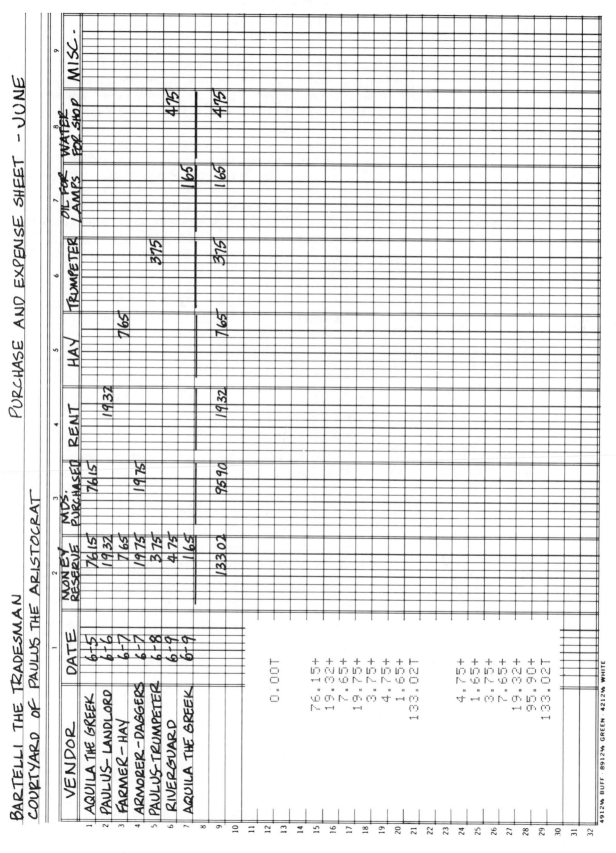

In order to show how this additional calculation will affect our income statement, we will make up a new one using the new figures. In taking inventory, remember that inventories are always calculated at cost value, not retail sales value.

If you have followed me this far in working out our small bookkeeping system, you will be able to take the results of a day's business, post them to your sales or cash-received sheet, and know how much money you have taken in for that day. You will also be able to post your paid-out sheets showing how much money has been spent and for what it was spent. You will also be able to take the totals of your daily journals, place them on a work sheet, and work up an income statement that will tell you accurately what your net profit is for that accounting period.

The next thing you will need is some form of accumulating sheet to bring the totals of all the months together in one form, from which the yearly income statement can be made without a big hassle. (Big business does this chore in their general ledger, and this will be explained later.)

<h1 style="text-align:center">Bartelli the Tradesman</h1>
<h2 style="text-align:center">Courtyard of Paulus the Aristocrat</h2>

Week June 5 through 12th

Income From Operations

Olive oil	$ 31.37	
Perfume	6.76	
Bolts of cloth	65.60	
Weapons	73.10	
Miscellaneous sales	10.05	
Total Sales		$186.88

Cost of Sales

Inventory—Beginning	$ 20.11	
Merchandise purchased	95.90	
Total Available for sale	$116.01	
Inventory—Ending	9.50	
Cost of merchandise sold		$106.51
Gross Profit from sales		$ 80.37

Operating Expenses

Rent to Paulus	$ 19.32	
Hay for horses	7.65	
Trumpeter to announce bargains	3.75	
Oil for shop lamps	1.65	
Water for shop	4.75	
Total cost of operating shop		$ 37.12
Net profit from operations		$ 43.25

Accumulating the Data

As the months went by and business continued to improve, Romulus realized that he had to have some form of record that would bring all of his work sheets together in one continuing set of accumulated totals. This way, at the end of the year, he wouldn't have to go back and add up all the various transactions again in order to know what his net profit was for the year.

Since Caesar was supporting many armies and purchasing much equipment, he was collecting taxes from all small trade shops. Romulus had to know how much profit his master had earned in order not to overpay his taxes.

In casting about for a method, he decided to take his income statement and simply add the figures of the following month to it. This gave him a total of the two months. When the third month had passed, he did the same procedure again, and had a total for three months. In order to show how this was done, I will draw figures out of my head to illustrate it. (All of my figures are arbitrary. We are interested in the method at this point, not actual figures.)

For example, suppose that we make up a set of figures for the month following our first income statement, which is July. For July, we will state that the shop had gross sales of $193.26, a cost of merchandise of $97.83, rent expense of $21.75, hay expense of $9.93, trumpeter expense of $4.60, oil for the shop expense of $2.21, and a water expense of $5.19.

By setting up our income statement like the first one, we find that we have a gross profit of $95.43. Expenses came to $43.68, and by subtracting this from the gross, we arrive at a net profit for that month of $51.75. By adding the net profits of the two months together, Romulus knows that he has a total net profit of $105.61.

He also wants to know what the totals of the individual items are for the two months so he decided to post the income items, the cost of sales, and the operating expense items next to the figures on the first sheet and add them all together.

After that was accomplished, his work sheet may have looked something like the one shown on the next page.

In the example of the income statement for June and July, we have an accumulative income statement which covers a period of two months. This is a simple method of accumulating two months but it still doesn't give an answer to the need for a means of accumulating statements for a full year.

In order to do this, Romulus added more sheets of paper to his statement, placing them side by side and adding his figures for each month as they came. In analyzing this form of accumulation, a system of posting figures to a sheet so that it can be carried from month to month has been worked out. This should not be confusing to the person who knows nothing about a general ledger. This system takes the place of the normal general ledger, and is simple enough for the person who has no education in accounting to understand.

Instead of adding sheets of paper together, like Romulus, we will obtain a columnar pad which contains twenty-one columns. This gives enough space to add several months together. It is much less expensive than setting up a normal general ledger, and will take the place of such a ledger until the business becomes so large that it is no longer practical.

So now we will make our ledger.

Bartelli the Tradesman
Courtyard of Paulus the Aristocrat
Statement—June 1 through July 31

Income	June		July		Total
Olive Oil	$ 31.37	+	$ 32.50	=	$ 63.87
Perfume	6.75	+	7.83	=	14.58
Bolts of cloth	65.60	+	67.30	=	132.90
Weapons	73.10	+	74.76	=	147.86
Other	10.05	+	10.87	=	20.92
Total Income	$186.88		$193.26		$380.14
Cost of Sales	95.90		97.83		193.73
Gross Profit	$90.98		$ 95.43		$186.41

Operating Expenses			
Rent to Paulus	$ 19.32	$ 21.75	$ 41.07
Hay Expense	7.65	9.93	17.58
Trumpeter Expense	3.75	4.60	8.35
Oil for lamps	1.65	2.21	3.86
Water for shop	4.75	5.19	9.94
Total Operating Expenses	$ 37.12	$ 43.68	$ 80.80
Net Profit from Operations	$ 53.86	$ 51.75	$105.61

The Ledger

On the first sheet of 11″ x 24″ 21-column pad, on the second line, write the word "Income." On the third line, write in the first item of your sales breakdown in the description space. Romulus would have written in his first item (olive oil). Skip a line. On the fifth line, write in the next sales item (for Romulus, this would have been "perfume." On the seventh line, he would have written "bolts of cloth," on the ninth line he would have written "weapons," and so forth.) "Other" would be on the thirteenth line, and the words "Total Sales" would be on line fifteen.

Skip a line. On line thirteen, write in the words "Cost of Sales." Skip a line. On line fifteen, write the first item of merchandise purchased. What this breakdown would be depends on your business and the amount of information you need in order to control the business. If you have various items for sale (such as leather goods, silver goods, women's apparel, shoes, and so forth), you might want to know the amount of each sold so you can tell whether stocking them is worthwhile. In that case, you would have to have a means of breaking down the sales in order to determine each one.

If you have no need for such a breakdown, simply write in the words "Cost of Sales."

After your last item, skip a line, write in "Total Cost of Sales." Skip a line. Write in "Operating Expenses." Skip a line. Start listing items of expenses which you will have. There will always be rent, utilities, telephone, insurance, advertising, auto or truck expenses, office supplies, etc. Leave a line between each item.

At the bottom of the page, leave two spaces and then enter "Total Operating Expenses." When you have finished making up your flatform ledger, it will follow the same format as the income statement, except that it is on an extra wide columnar sheet of paper.

Now mark the columns on the sheet of paper. Starting at the left, skip three columns and draw a line with black or blue pencil from top to bottom. In the boxes above the columns, write "Sales Sheet" (or cash received) in the first column. In the second column, write "Paid Outs" (or check register). In the third column, write "Total." On the line above the boxes, write "June," or the first month of business that is to be recorded.

Filling In the Numbers

When the sheets are completed (it will probably take two or three), write in all of the account totals from the bottom of your work sheets or journals. Then place the totals of the items, added across from left to right, in the total column. This is the total for the first month, and will be the same as the statement for the first month, if we are posting the figures from Romulus' work sheets.

Next count off four columns and draw a line down the column line in black or blue pencil. In the boxes above the column, print in "Sales" (or cash received), "Paid Outs" (check distribution), "Total for the Month," and in the fourth column, write "Total to Date." When the next month's business is completed, enter the word "July," or the month of business you are currently in. Then add them for the "Month Total." Then add that total to the June total for a "Total to Date."

By adding all of the item totals across, as we did on the income statements, what we have is an income statement which is becoming larger and larger through accumulating the figures from each monthly statement. The business owner can know at any time what gross sales are, what cost of sales is, and what net profit is. Such a system could even be added to, at the end of the week, if there should be a reason for doing so. It is up to the person doing the posting to make certain that the proper items are posted to the proper columns.

So now we have a very simple bookkeeping system on the cash method of reporting earnings for tax purposes. We also have a ledger which is as easy to post and read as the sample income statement made up by Romulus.

However, perfect as it is for the very small business that has few changes over long periods of time, it would be unsuitable for the larger business that is continually growing and adding more accounts. Figures 3. and 4. are examples of the flatform ledger or accumulating sheets which will work very well for your small business.

In making up the accumulative sheets for Hazel's Gift Shop, I have added together only the months of June and July. The same procedure is followed through for all the other months of the year. Only at the end of the year is it discontinued and a new set of sheets made. This is

Figure 3

HAZEL'S GIFT SHOP — GENERAL LEDGER
SANTA CRUZ, CA — JUNE

	CASH RECEIVED (SALES)	PAID OUTS (CK. DIST.)	TOTAL	CASH RECEIVED (SALES)	PAID OUTS (CK. DIST.)	TOTAL		TOTAL TO DATE	
	1	2	3	4	5	6	7	8	9
INCOME									
LEATHER GOODS	47595		47595	51920		51920		99515	
APPAREL	37322		37322	25737		25737		63059	
SHOES	29586		29586	15607		15607		45193	
COSMETICS	27319		27319	9975		9975		37294	
TOTAL SALES			141822			103239		245061	
COST OF SALES									
MERCHANDISE PURCHASE		78005	78005		56781	56781		134786	
FREIGHT IN		2660	2660		1793	1793		4453	
TOTAL COST OF SALES			80665		58574			139239	
GROSS PROFIT			61157			44665		105822	
OPERATING EXPENSES									
ADVERTISING EXPENSE		1723	1723		1690	1690		3413	
RENT EXPENSE		8900	8900		8900	8900		17800	
TELEPHONE EXP.		1563	1563		1415	1415		2978	
INSURANCE EXP.		12500	12500		—	—		12500	
UTILITIES EXP.		1923	1923		1850	1850		3773	

49121⁄2 BUFF · 89121⁄2 GREEN · 42121⁄2 WHITE

Figure 4

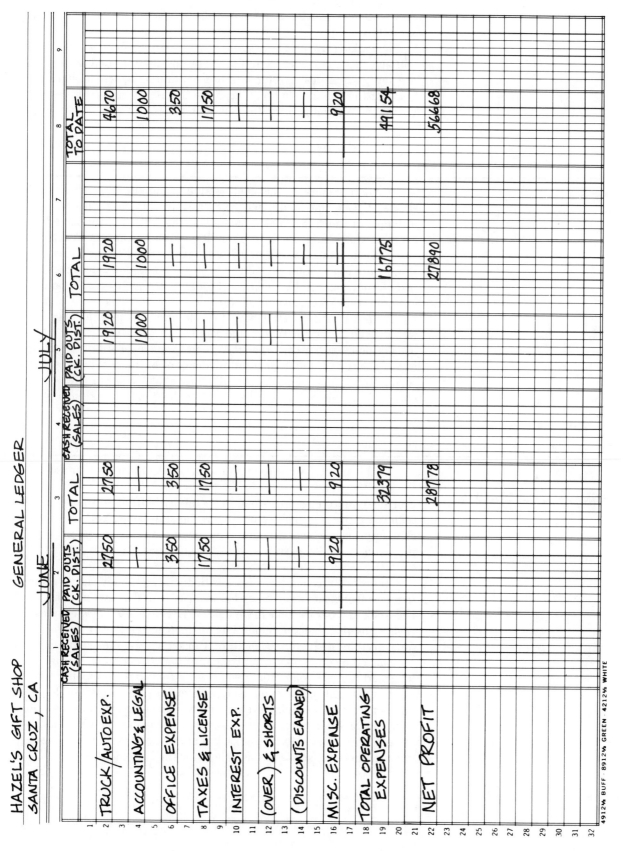

because we enter a new accounting year (except in the case of a corporation, which sometimes uses fiscal years), and must start from scratch.

In making up future accumulative sheets (general ledger), there will be other items included. These are not discontinued at the end of the year, but are carried forward in a continuing figure throughout the years of the company's life. These are the assets and liabilities of the company. We will go into them in later pages.

Sales Tax

Also, in making up the sales section of the gift shop accumulative sheets, I have not mentioned sales tax. In this case, this would be included in the total sales, since all of the gift shop merchandise is taxable. This would not be true for all types of businesses. A vegetable stand, for instance, would be all non-taxable if all of the items at the stand were food products. (Check local state laws for determination of taxable and non-taxable items.) If the stand carried flowers or plants, for example, those items would be taxable in some states.

A grocery store would have taxable and non-taxable items, and would need a system that would keep such sales separated. This is usually done with a cash register which keeps a record of the taxable items, the tax paid on them, and the amount of the non-taxable items. Again, for the sake of clarity, we will defer exploring such sales until we enter the double entry cash basis of bookkeeping for tax purposes.

The Financial Statement

At this point, I want to mention one of the most profound woes of the small business owner. This is the financial statement. Nothing has ever been more misunderstood or so totally baffling to the lay person than the process of making up a financial statement. Yet, taken in the slow approach which Romulus had been using, a statement can be prepared by the lay person with a little guidance. To show you just how simple it is, let's do one right now.

In order to have a basis for our financial statement, let us assume that Hazel of Hazel's Gift Shop has a desire to add a new line of goods to her stock in order to make more money. Because it is a new business, it is very possible that she cannot buy on open account and must pay cash for everything delivered to her store. Consequently, she needs money to purchase the new stock. In applying for a loan at her bank, she has been informed that the loan officer will need a financial statement.

In the usual course of a business enterprise, the owner will have set up his or her bookkeeping system and will have records of transactions from the very beginning of the business. The values we will need have already been entered in the books, but not so with Hazel. We will have to question her and arrive at our values for the statement.

Assets

The first section of the statement is the "Assets." Assets are the nice things that happen in a business. So we will put down the first item of importance—money.

In making up a financial statement (see Figure 5.), money is classified as cash in the bank, with the name of your bank (Bank of America, California Bank, Staten Island Bank, or whatever bank you are using). A merchant could have money in several. If so, each one would be shown. But we will assume that Hazel keeps all of her money in just one bank, and we will use the Bank of America as an example.

In the upper left-hand corner, under the heading of "Assets," we will write in the words "Cash in Bank—Bank of America," and place the amount of money Hazel had in the bank at the end of the last month, or at the end of the statement month. This amount, we will assume, was $673.68. This will be placed on the right-hand side of the statement sheet, opposite the heading "Cash in Bank."

Inventory

Under assets, the second item on the report would be *inventory*. In making up the income statement, we stated that Hazel didn't have an inventory. For the sake of procedure, let's say that she did. Unless she has a method of keeping a perpetual inventory, we have to assume that she counted the merchandise physically in order to arrive at an accurate cost figure. We will accept her word that the amount of inventory was $496.73, and will place it on the right-hand side of the paper opposite the heading "Inventory."

Equipment

Hazel doesn't make deliveries, but she does sometimes purchase at wholesale houses. She has a small Datsun pickup truck which she purchased second-hand for $976.83. We will place this figure under the Inventory figure and call it *equipment*.

Fixtures & Furniture

In starting her shop, Hazel found it necessary to purchase some second-hand showcases and counters. This provided a means of displaying her wares to an advantage and still protecting them from shoplifters. She was able to locate several good display cases and two unusual tables, which she was able to purchase for $1,800.00 We will place that figure after the heading *fixtures and furniture*.

Office Equipment

Every business person needs a means of writing business letters so that they look professional. Hazel purchased a typewriter for $79.85 and an adding machine for $69.75. This gives her a total of $149.60 for *office equipment,* and we will place this in the column with the other values.

Total Assets

Now that we have all the figures for the cash on hand, the inventory, equipment and fixtures, we can add them up and arrive at a total value of the store's assets, which is $4,096.94. We will now draw a line under the last item and place the total below it. This is called "Total Assets." This concludes our assets section.

Liabilities

Next, we will prepare the *liabilities* section. These are negative things in a business. The assets are usually called the debits, and the liabilities are called the credits. I prefer to call them the positive and negative items.

Accounts Payable

The first item to be entered in the liabilities section is the amount of money owed by the business for purchases that have not yet been paid. This is called the *Accounts Payable.* These will be discussed to a greater length in a later section of the book. At this particular point, however, we will assume that Hazel paid cash for all of her merchandise and does not owe on any. (We are on a cash basis of accounting and there can not be unpaid invoices in this system.) We will enter a "zero" on the statement behind the heading of Accounts Payable, or leave it off altogether.

Loans Payable

When Hazel purchased the Datsun truck, she didn't have enough money, so she borrowed $300.00 from her bank. She will pay it back at the rate of $25.00 per month. Place $300.00 *immediately* following the heading of *Loans Payable—Truck* (see example).

In purchasing the fixtures and furniture, Hazel put a down payment of $1,000.00 and promised to pay the balance of $800.00 at the rate of $100.00 per month. We will write in the word *Fixtures* in the descriptions space and follow it with the total of $800.00 (under the $300.00 for the truck). Now we will add the two figures and carry the total to the right-hand column under the other figures. The total is $1,100.00.

Total Current Liabilities

Since we have no loan figure for the typewriter and adding machine, we can assume that Hazel paid cash for these. We can write down our heading *Total Current Liabilities,* draw a line under the figures we have placed on our work sheet, and add them up. We now have the total of $1,100.00 in the "total" space below the line after the heading "Current Liabilities."

Our next item is *Capital*. In starting a business, every business person must have some cash in order to pay the rent on a building, purchase stock, buy equipment, and pay for other necessities. Hazel placed money in her bank with which to pay the first month's rent, buy the merchandise, install a telephone, and so forth. Pretending that we have no means of getting this information from her (this happens all the time), let's put down what information we do have and work back to the bank deposit amount. This will be done through subtracting from the amount of the total liabilities.

Capital

This brings us face-to-face with a factor we have not yet mentioned in working up our bookkeeping system. The factor? In accounting, *assets always equal liabilities*. This is one of life's little laws that may not make perfect sense to you, but is always true under all circumstances. It simply means that for every positive thing, there is a negative thing. Or, for every value maintained in the assets section, there is a corresponding value in the liabilities section. This means that if the inventory (if any) and the equipment and the fixtures and the office supplies were all suddenly turned into cash, the store would retain none of it. Every dime would have to be allocated to some other thing or being. All you have to remember right now is that the liabilities of a business *will always equal the assets* of that business. We will dig into this a bit deeper in a later example.

Okay, so now you know that.

So, we are short one of the important amounts of money, but we have the means of working it out. In order to do that, we will place the amount of the Total Liabilities at the bottom of the work sheet. This is $4,096.94. We know this because $4,096.94 is the amount of Total Assets, and assets-always-equal-liabilities, right?

Assets = Liabilities

From that amount we will deduct a few things to get us back to the original deposit made by Hazel. Just below the total of the current liabilities ($1,100.00), on the left-hand side of the sheet, place the word "CAPITAL" in capital letters. A couple of spaces underneath it, place the words "Capital and Proprietorship." Underneath that, pencil in the words "Cash Investment." This is the figure we are looking for and will be able to fill in later.

Underneath the investment, write in the amounts that were paid down on the truck and the fixtures. The amount, $676.83, and the $1,000.00 are both additional capital contributions and must be entered here. Then add them up, draw a line, and write the total of $1,676.83. Add to that total the amount of net profit from sales for the two months ($566.68). (We are assuming that is as long as Hazel has been in business for this statement.) Now add the $1,676.83 and the $566.68 together. We now have a total of $2,243.51. This is the total of known capital and the retained earnings.

Cash Investment

Place the "Total Liabilities" figure ($4,096.94) in your adding machine and deduct from it the $1,100.00 of the current liabilities. This leaves a balance of $2,996.94 as the owner's equity in the business. Now, from this figure, deduct $2,243.51, and this will give you a balance of $753.43. This is the amount of money Hazel placed in the bank to start her business. If this confuses you, hang in there, we'll go through all of it again at another time.

You can work the same figures another way by placing the total liabilities figure (the same as total assets, remember?) in the adding machine and subtracting from it the current liabilities figure ($1,100.00). This leaves a balance of $2,996.94. From this, subtract the amount of retained earnings ($566.68), then the amount paid for the fixtures ($1,000.00), the amount paid down on the truck ($676.83) and total them. This leaves the amount of $753.43, or the original cash investment.

Now it is necessary to add the capital figures again, so place the investment figure in the column in the space left for it, and add the three figures together. This time, we get a total of $2,430.26 instead of the original $1,676.51. Add the new figure ($2,430.26) to the retained earnings figure, and the new total will be the owner's equity in the business ($2,996.94).

The Drawing Account

In ninety percent of small business enterprises, the owner will take some money out of it for his or her own use as a full or partial income. The money taken from the business, whether taken in cash from the cash register or by writing a check from the checkbook, is termed a *draw*. This is not money earned and taxes are not paid on it.

If a person put twenty thousand dollars into a business the first year, then drew out ten thousand dollars as a draw, all that is being done is taking back the owner's money to live on. However, if the owner puts in only ten thousand dollars and then draws out twenty thousand dollars, he has taken back his own money plus ten thousand dollars of the vendor's money. In fact, he has used money to live on that is not his.

If Hazel had drawn out an amount of money, we would have taken it from the check record and posted it to her drawing account. It would have shown up in the capital section below the retained earnings, and would be deducted from the totals to that point.

Let us assume that Hazel did draw out $500.00 This amount would be posted under the total of the capital and retained earnings ($2,996.94) and subtracted from it, leaving a new equity of $2,496.94. This amount ($500.00) must also be subtracted from the Cash account. We will take this up in more detail in the next section of this book, which is the double entry cash method of accounting for taxes.

As we stand now, you have learned how to work up a set of records for the small shop and have made up an income statement and balance sheet. When a bank asks for a balance sheet, it usually also includes the income statement. It is now time to expand our system to handle the methods of business other than cash sales.

Figure 5.

**Hazel Hayworth
DBA
Hazel's Gift Shop
921 Hazelwood Drive
Santa Cruz, California**

Balance Sheet

July 31, 19_____

Assets

Cash in Bank—Bank of America	$ 173.78
Inventory—Merchandise	496.73
Equipment	976.83
Furniture & Fixtures	1,800.00
Office Equipment	149.60
Total Assets	$3,596.94

Liabilities

Accounts Payable		$ -0-
Loans Payable		
Truck	$ 300.00	
Fixtures	800.00	1,100.00
Total Current Liabilities		$1,100.00

Capital

Capital & Proprietorship		
Investments	$ 753.43	
Additional Capital Contributed		
Used for downpayment on Truck	676.83	
Used for fixtures	1,000.00	
Total Investments	$2,430.26	
Retained Earnings	566.68	
	$2,996.94	
Hazel Hayworth—Drawing	500.00	
Equity in Business		$2,496.94
Total Liabilities and Net Worth		$3,596.94

Now that you have learned the basis of a single entry, cash method of accounting for your business, it is time to expand on it and develop it into an accounting system that will give you a complete record of the transaction of the business.

We will call it our "Double Entry, Cash Method of Accounting for Tax Purposes."

A common question to be answered at this point is, "What is the difference between bookkeeping and accounting?" The bookkeeper usually does the daily routine of posting to the daily journals or work sheets. The accountant takes the daily work at the end of the month, posts it to the general ledger, and makes up the income and financial statements.

Now, aren't you glad you know all that?

3

The Beginning of a Double Entry Cash Method of Accounting for Tax Purposes

Hello! Glad to see you back!

Now that you have followed me this far, we will begin a probe of the double entry accounting system so that you will know what it is, why it is necessary, and how to begin working with it.

Double entry bookkeeping or accounting is not all the big bug-a-boo that some people would have you believe. Double entry accounting is just that—double entry—and you enter each figure twice. But here I will explain that you may not be entering the identical figure on each side of the books. Sometimes you will be entering a combination of figures that will add up to the original figure.

For example, suppose we write a check, take the money out of the bank, and pay three bills with the cash. When we posted that check to our check register, it would look something like this:

Credits			Debits		
Bank	Description		Utilities	Gasoline	Advertising
130.00	Cash		30.00	25.00	75.00

(Remember that this is strictly an example and it might never happen this way unless you cashed the check and paid the bills with the cash.) But we entered the sum of $130.00 as a credit to the bank account and debited the other accounts for a total of $130.00. We entered the same (actual) figure twice. Or perhaps I should say that we entered the same *Value* twice. This is double entry.

Credits and Debits

Double entry books have two sides; the credits and the debits. Before I confuse you any more, let's examine a few of Romulus' entries to show how he posted them to his double entry work sheets. (We will forget the credit and debit terminology for the time being, and just examine the entries.)

As sales increased, Romulus had customers come into the shop who were good friends of his master. They were permitted to take merchandise for which they promised to pay later. In order to show his master that the sale had been made but that no money had been received, he had to make up charge slips that could be deducted from the total of the overall sales. This was to prove the amount of money he had in the cash box. Because such sales were usually small, a small sheet of paper was enough to write down the few items that had been purchased in this manner. He wrote the name of the item with the price of each so that he could have a total of the entire transaction. He called such slips "credits" because they were part of the total sales for that day.

Sales Slips

At the end of the day, Romulus would add up the totals of his sales slips and know immediately how much money was supposed to be in his cash box. In writing up his sales slips, he had to mark each one as to whether it was a credit or cash sale and then segregate them at the end of the day. He did this before adding the totals and posting the figures in his daily journal.

Romulus' sales slips might have appeared somewhat like the following examples:

Figure 6.

Bartelli the Tradesman
Courtyard of Paulus the Aristocrat
June 15, 100 AD

Lady Apollo
Inn of the Seven Veils
Rome, Italy

		Charge Sale
1	Urn Goat's Milk	$ 1.23
1	Bolt Silk Cloth	4.76
2	Vials Perfume @ $1.85	3.70
1	Brass-tip Shield	14.95
	Total Sale	$24.64
	Sales Tax	1.40
	Sale Including Tax	26.04

Figure 7.

Bartelli the Tradesman
Courtyard of Paulus the Aristocrat
June 15, 100 AD

Cash Sale

3 Split-quill Penns @ $.65		$ 1.95
1 Vase of Olive Oil		7.75
1 Dagger		3.59
1 Leather Shield		9.95
Total Sale		$23.24
Sales Tax		.93
Sales Including Tax		$24.17

Now we will post these sales to our new double entry work sheet which we will make up from the same columnar pad which we used for the single entry sales journal. Such posting will look something like the example shown in Figure 8.

In examining the new double entry journal, you will notice that the description column is the dividing line of our new work sheet and that the figures have been entered twice. We have posted the kind of sales (cash or charge) on the left-hand side, and the type of sale (taxable or non-taxable) on the right-hand side. Each group of figures or variations of the figures (totals) has been posted on each side of the work sheet.

This takes care of the manner in which a charge sale is posted and how the cash sale is posted. The clerk will know how much money is needed to reconcile with the money on hand to make up the deposit. The owner must know how much tax is owed so that it can be remitted to the state whenever the tax form is due. Now is a good time to bring this matter into focus.

The sale to Lady Apollo consists almost entirely of merchandise, with only one item that is food. Usually, food is the only item that is non-taxable. In order to calculate the sales tax, Romulus deducted the amount of the goat's milk and figured tax on the balance. Total Sale, $24.64, less goat's milk, $1.23, equals taxable sale, $23.41. He multiplied that figure times the amount of the 6% tax. (It is 6% in California, but it will vary, depending upon the state.) Six percent times $23.41 gave him a tax of $1.40 and a total of $26.04, entered on our new work sheet.

Romulus took the cash sale, Figure 7, and did the same thing with it. With a total of $23.24, less the vase of olive oil (used in cooking), he had a balance of $15.49. The figure (the taxable amount) times 6% equals $.93, which is the tax. Added to the old total of $23.24, a new total of $24.17 was entered on the new work sheet.

Figure 8.

Bartelli the Tradesman
Courtyard of Paulus the Aristocrat

Double Entry Sales Journal—August

	(Over) Short	Charge Accounts	Money Box	Description	Non-Taxable	Taxable Sales	Sales Tax
		26.04		Lady Apollo	1.23	23.41	1.40
			24.17		7.75	15.49	.93
Totals		26.04	24.17		8.98	38.90	2.33

To prove our new double entry system of bookkeeping, add each line across and you will find that the sales on the right equal the amount posted in the left-hand part of the work sheet. By adding up each column, the non-taxable totals $8.98, the taxable sales total $38.90, and the amount of sales tax collected is $2.33. Add the totals across, and we find that the totals of the sales side equal $50.21. The total of the left side is also $50.21. The sales journal is in balance.

What It All Means

This is double entry bookkeeping. We enter every figure twice, either in amount or in variations of the amount. Then when we add up the columns at the end of the month, the sum of the left side totals will equal the sum of the totals on the right side. If they do not, then there has been a mistake.

Single entry bookkeeping does not show errors. There might be a very large mistake in a single entry system, and the bookkeeper would never know it.

So now we have learned how to handle our cash sales, charge sales, and taxable and non-taxable sales. It is now time to see what can happen when Romulus counts the money in his box and discovers that it isn't all there. In handling some of his cash transactions during the day's business, he has made some errors in making change and is now short of money in his box. (This also happens frequently in the cash register.)

Overs and Shorts

In setting up a bookkeeping system for the small shop, it is advisable to have an "over and short" column and keep track of the money that is lost or accumulated this way. It is a simple procedure and one that needs only one more column on our double entry sales journal. In the fluctuations of overs and shorts, the business might come up a few dollars short each month. This is counted as an expense, and is posted in the operating expenses.

To create an example, we will suppose that Romulus has counted his money for the day, checked it against his sales slips (or cash register tapes) and finds he is one dollar and thirty-seven cents short. When he posts his figures on his work sheet, he does it as usual but also posts that shortage in the over/short column. When this amount is added to the amount he is putting in his box the total will equal the total of his sales. When posting the overage/shortage in the column, the overage is bracketed ( ) so that it is known it is an overage and is deducted from the cash in the box in order to equal the sales figure.

When the time comes to total the column, enter the bracketed figures in your adding machine as a minus and the unbracketed figures a as a plus. Accountants name this process "footing a column." If the footing comes out as a minus, bracket it and post the amount in the general ledger with brackets. A plus footing will be posted without brackets. What this means is that a bracketed item in an expense category signifies a reduction to that expense that results in an increase in net profit. But, another way of looking at overages is to realize that someone, probably a customer, has been shortchanged.

Accounting for the Draw

Now let's go on to another account item which is always a part of the bookkeeping of any business—the owner's draw. Since the owner is in business to make a living, from time to time the owner must draw funds from the business in order to pay personal bills and take care of dependents. This "taking money" from the flow of business cash is called his "drawing account" and is kept in an account column (or page) of its own in the general ledger. Usually such withdrawals are made by writing a check. It is picked up in the posting of the check register (and we will cover this topic in the check-distribution section). The owner's draw could also show up in the sales or cash-received sheet. This happens when the owner runs into the shop, scoops a handful of bills from the register, tosses a piece of scratch paper into the drawer and yells, "I took $25. I put it on a slip." Then when you count the cash, you find the slip.

Let's assume the store had sales of $175.65 for the day. When you counted the money that night, or the next morning, all you find is $148.67.

In reconciling the cash from the register, or sales slips, you discover that you are short $26.98. Now you deduct the owner's withdrawal of $25 from the amount you are short. This leaves you with a balance of $1.98. Let's post this as a shortage to our new sales sheet and see what it looks like in Figure 9.

In order to view the scope of our new worksheet in posting the few forms of transactions we have already learned, we will post a new monthly sheet for Hazel's Gift Ship for the month of August. On it we will show the various sales and the tax collected on the credit side (right-hand side of the sales sheet). The cash received or accounted for will be posted on the debit side (left-hand side of the sales sheet).

On the debit side, we will post the cash in the box, the amount of charge sales, Hazel's withdrawals from the cash register, amounts that were paid out for merchandise or expenses, and the over/short column.

Figure 9

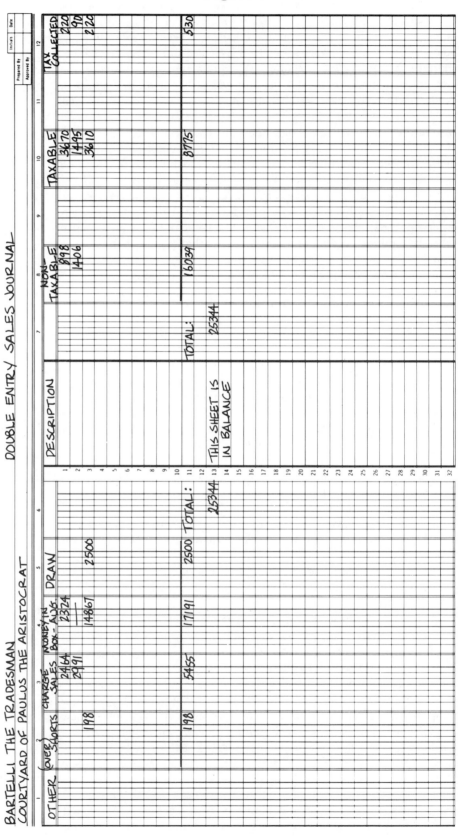

In making up this new work sheet, I have shown entries for only five days. It is to be continued for the full month in the same manner shown in Figure 10.

I have posted arbitrary figures to the various items in order to illustrate the manner in which it is done. I have then added each line across so that I have a total with which to reconcile when I add the lines on the opposite side of the sheet. These totals are the amounts of money that were supposedly collected for that day for the merchandise and tax transactions. When we post the amount of money that is in the box, enter the amount of credit sales (charge sales) from our sales slips, then enter the money taken for cash paid-outs and Hazel's personal needs, we have either a shortage or an overage for that day or we are in balance.

When all of this has been posted, added across, and checked so that the left side of each line reconciles with the right side, we can add up the individual columns and put the total below that column. When all columns are totaled, we add the total across and compare the totals. If they equal as they do in Figure 10, the sheet is in balance down to that point.

Checking For Errors

A good bookkeeper will always add up the columns at least once a week so that he/she can check the balance and be able to correct it. This is to discover errors and correct them before they become compounded. It is much easier to keep the columns in balance if they are added frequently.

Practice

To help you understand what has happened on this work sheet, I suggest that you play with it. Make up transactions of your own and post them to the same type of sheet. The columnar pad is so inexpensive that you can afford to throw away a number of sheets. By practicing with sales, you will become more adept at recognizing the different kinds of sales and how to post them. When you get into the process of setting up your own books, you will have a good working knowledge of what you are doing.

Have you followed this far? Good! Now we can explore our new double entry bookkeeping system of accounting by the cash method for the small business.

Now that we have examined the double entry system of accounting and have been shown how it affects businesses, we will proceed into working up a system which will be most beneficial to your own business. We want a system which leaves the least possibility for error. But it must also give an accurate picture of what your sales and profits are for any given period of time.

Figure 10

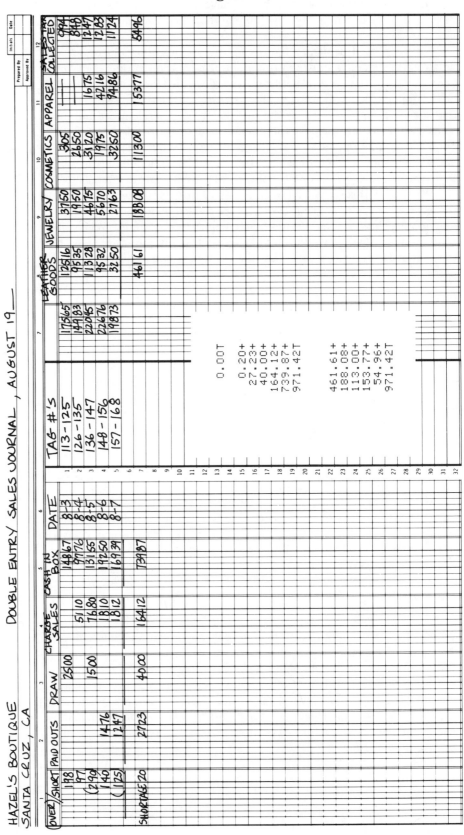

4

Your Accounting System

Thanks for coming this far. I know it wasn't easy, and that you had your doubts along the way. But now that you are here, you will undoubtedly be able to finish this section and know what setting up a bookkeeping system for your business involves.

It takes a little intelligence and a whole lot of determination. But the first thing you know, the job is completed and you are posting your daily work as if you had been doing it for the last twenty years. Then when you post the monthly totals to your flatform ledger and discover that you actually made money for the month, you will know that the project was worth every moment you spent on it.

There are high-priced accountants sweating over adding machines who couldn't have done a better job than you did all by yourself. I think that calls for congratulations.

To prove that all of this jubilation hasn't been in vain, let's set up a new sales sheet, make up a thriving entity and a post a sales month. This new form combines cash with sales and illustrates a variation of the necessity to have the left hand side equal the right. As you examine Figure 11, you will see how the sheet still provides a balancing technique.

Since we already have Hazel's Gift Shop, let's update it, give it a new name, and post a month of transactions. This will give you an idea of what a full month looks like.

Being a small, cottage-type enterprise like those found on the streets of any small town, Hazel's is operated solely as a husband/wife combination. The husband works full time somewhere else while Hazel takes care of the shop. Since all of the merchandise she sells is taxable, to collect the tax and report her liability to the state, she will post a "tax collected" column. To calculate the correct amount of tax on each item sold, Hazel or her sales clerk will use one of the charts provided by most states.

As you begin your business, you may not want to advance credit to any customers until you have more experience. So, if all your sales will be on a cash and carry basis, Figure 11 can be used to record both sales and their effect on cash. Later you will find Figure 12 which illustrates the same type of transactions with allowances for charge or credit sales.

Assume we will be working from sales tags which have been made up by you or your sales clerk. These show the item sold, the price, the sales tax, and the total of the sale. In working with the tags, you will want to total them in order to have a control figure. Tags will then be segregated into the various types of sales. The segregated tags can then be added and the totals entered in the columns which apply on Figure 11. If more than one type of merchandise is on one sales slip, you or your bookkeeper will have to re-cap them on a scratch sheet before entering the information.

How It Will Look

Refer to Figure 11 now and we will examine the entries and see how you can produce the same type of record in your business. This form combines sales figures with cash paid out and an ending figure which should be what you have deposited into your bank account the next day.

Each day's sales will be shown on one line. If you would like to control the sales tag numbers to make sure none has been lost or misapplied, you can use the unmarked wide column following the date to indicate the beginning and ending tag numbers. The columns headed "**Apparel**," "**Leather**," "**Jewelry**," and "**Footwear**" can be noted to display whatever type of sales your business will develop. For Hazel's Boutique, we see that September 2nd's sales were made up of $175.10 in **Apparel**, $165.29 in **Leather**, $210.20 in **Jewelry**, and $116.69 in **Footwear**. The total of all sales, shown in the next column, is $667.28 for that day. In this instance, we are assuming the state has a sales tax of 6% and that amount, $40.04, is entered in the next column to the right. On the same day, Hazel also borrowed $500. for the business and that is entered and noted accordingly.

The next column to the right indicates the total of all the cash taken in that day. Adding across the total of all sales, $667.28; the sales tax collected, $40.04; the loan of $500.; we find a total cash taken in of $1,207.32. If there had been no pay outs and no errors in handling cash, that amount would have been deposited directly into the bank the next day. We find, however, that Hazel withdrew for her personal use $100., and she was short by $3. in reconciling her cash drawer at the end of the day. So, there is $103. recorded as **Cash Paid Out—Total** in the second column from the far right. This $103. is deducted from the total cash taken in, $1,207.32, and the resultant figure of $1,104.32 will be deposited into the bank. If you use this type of form, you will find good control of your sales, your tax liability for sales tax collected and your daily cash position. If you would like to do so, you can use the other side of the form to analyze the amounts entered for **Cash Paid Out—Other.**

On September 3rd, from the total cash taken in of $1,113.53, Hazel paid out $210., probably for merchandise, and she experienced a cash overage of $26. This latter amount is deducted from the $210. pay out (because it actually is cash IN) and the net figure of $184. is a deduction from the $1,113.53 to arrive at the amount to be deposited.

Figure 11 shows only five working days of activity simply to illustrate how the form is to be used. In pratice each line would record one day's activity, and the columns would be added down and proofs would be derived in this way. The totals of all the **Sales** columns would be added to the **Sales Tax** column total and to the **Other Cash**

Figure 11

HAZEL'S BOUTIQUE CASH AND SALES JOURNAL SEPTEMBER, 19__
SANTA CRUZ, CA

DATE	SALES Apparel	Leather	Jewelry	Footwear	Total	Sales Tax	Other Amount Loan	Cash Amount	Total Cash In	Draw	Cash Paid Out Other	Over/Short	Total	Cash Into Bank
2	11510	11652	21000	11164	126728	4004		50000	120132	10000		300	11300	111432
3	11925	21620	43500	20005	109050	6303			111353		21000	(2400)	18400	92953
4	7520	10003	20054	9525	47102	2826			49928		15200	425	15625	34303
5	22000	30000	61925	11929	125854	7551			133405		25200		25000	108405
		60455	146449	53128	344734	20684		50000	415418	10000	61200	(1875)	69325	346043

Amount column total to prove to the total of the **Total Cash In** column. And so on across the page.

In studying this latest adventure into sales accounting, I wouldn't doubt that you consider the example to be a very complicated sheet. It really isn't. If you had posted it one day at a time, day after day throughout the month, each day's posting would have been simple. It is only when you look at the finished product that it appears to be mind-boggling.

How Mistakes Are Made

I must confess that I didn't intend to make the over and short column come out with such a large overage amount. But in posting the figures from my head, then adding them up with one finger on the adding machine while tracing the column with another, I missed a key and made a ten-dollar error in one of the sales totals. This created a large shortage for that day.

This error might never have been discovered if we were not working a double entry accounting system. The sheet did not balance the first time I tried and so I knew something was wrong. In this instance, it was only a small amount, but in other circumstances it could have had costly results. This one example is enough to prove the worth of the double entry bookkeeping system.

This breakdown system is necessary if you want information that will show how your sales are running. If one kind of merchandise is not moving fast enough, it might be best to discard it and use the space for items which will sell more rapidly.

The Receivables

As your business increases, if you permit charge or credit business, it will be necessary to set up some means of keeping track of such sales and payments for them. This is usually done by having the customer sign a sales slip. You will probably want to make up a small file card on which you write the customer's name, address, place of work, phone number, and other bits of information you might need. The item sold and the amount of the total sale can be written on the card and filed in a small "receivable file" which can be checked periodically. The signed sales slip is usually filed in an alphabetized file folder so that it can be found readily when the customer comes in to pay. Then it can be filed away with the month's business.

This is the beginning of a "receivable file" (subsidiary ledger) necessary as the business embarks on credit transactions. Take a good look at Figure 12, which is used in a fashion identical to Figure 11 with variations to allow you to record your charge sales and their related sales tax, if any.

September 2nd's activity indicates all sales as follows: $152.20 in **Apparel,** $21.50 in **Leather,** $32.10 in **Jewelry** and $14.95 in **Footwear.** These amounts have been derived by you or your sales clerk by analyzing those sales tags and slips. In preparing this entry, I have shown the entire $152.20 for **Apparel** sales as though they were on credit. The sales tax of 6% on this amount is $9.13, and it is added to the sales of $152.20. The total of $161.33 is shown in the column, **Accounts Receivable.** We also enter the $9.13 sales tax in the **Sales Tax Charge** column. Obviously, you will have one or more sales slips with customers' names, addresses, etc. to support this entry, and these slips will total $161.33, since you must have added in the sales tax. The remainder of the sales for September 2nd total $68.55, which is shown in the Cash column next to **Accounts Receivable.** The sales tax on $68.55, if 6%, is $4.11, which is entered in the appropriate column after having been collected at the time of the sale.

Also on this day, Hazel borrowed $1,000 from the bank for deposit to the business account. The remainder of the form parallels Figure 11 with one addition. We must record the event of customers paying their outstanding balances.

As with **Cash Paid Out—Other,** you may use the reverse side to record the names of customers who have asked for or paid on credit sales. This information will also appear on your sales slips when the transactions occur.

Finally, you will see that proof of this form can be brought about in this manner. Totals of the columns for **Sales—Cash, Sales Tax—Cash, Paid on Account,** and **Other Cash—Amount** will agree with that of **Total Cash In.** Since this form does not provide a column to total sales, you will want to use some other available space on the form to indicate that day's total sales, if that figure will be of interest to you.

Now let's go on to the "paid-outs sheet" or "check distribution," as it is normally called. See Figure 13.

When Romulus, our Roman slave, made up his cash received sheet, he put all of his money in a box so that it would be handy to prove to his master that he had the proper amount. Such a method would be difficult today. Instead, we have established banking systems which are both convenient and which safeguard our money. Instead of showing our deposits to be "in the box," we can now change the name to "in the bank," or simply "bank." This is the way it is shown on sales and cash-received sheets.

Figure 12

HAZEL'S BOUTIQUE
SANTA CRUZ, CA

CASH AND SALES JOURNAL   SEPTEMBER, 19___

| | SALES | | | | SALES | | SALES TAX | | PAID ON | OTHER | CASH | TOTAL CASH | CASH PAID OUT | | | | CASH | |
DATE	APPAREL	LEATHER	JEWELRY	FOOTWEAR	ACCOUNTS RECEIVABLE	CASH	CHARGE	CASH	ACCOUNT	ACCOUNT	AMOUNT	IN	DRAW	OTHER	SHORT/OVER	TOTAL	INTO BANK	
2	15220	21150	3210	1495	16133	6855	913	411		LOAN	100000	107266	12500		126	26226	104640	
3	9576	47150	21175	2983	10151	17108	575	594	5310			15812	10000	1620		11620	81972	
4	12568	82190	3250	31115	8787	18928	447	1136	6225			26288		15000	(310)	14690	15599	
5	9261	7592	97150	1995	12450	16863	705	1011				17864		2210		2210	15654	
6																		
7																		
8																		
9																		
10																		
11																		
12																		
13																		
14																		
15																		
16																		
17																		
18																		
19																		
20																		
21																		
22																		
23																		
24																		
25																		
26																		
27																		
28																		
29																		
30	363323	171929	63602	38212	47521	592255	2690	35373	11535		100000	734143	12500	188636	(94)	31146	707777	

The Checking Account

When Romulus accepted deliveries from vendors, he took money out of his cash box to pay them. We do the same thing today. However, we have a different and safer means of taking money out of the cash box. Since it might be several blocks away and we wouldn't want to run to the bank for a withdrawal of a few dollars every time we wanted to pay a bill, we do it by means of a check.

The Cash Register

This is a very simple way of dispensing funds. We can do it without moving from our desk chair in the shop. When writing a check, mark on the stub what the payment is for, the invoice number, the vendor's name, and cash discount (if any). This information can then be written into our check distribution, Figure 13, which replaces Romulus' paid-out sheet. Despite the difference in payment method, the paid-outs are handled in the same manner as they were when our slave friend took money from his cash box and marked the amount down on his improvised sheet.

Freight Costs

In looking over Figure 13, you will note that I have posted five items to the merchandise purchased account. Four of the checks are made out to distributors with whom Hazel deals, while one of them is made out to the J & S Trucking Company. This is for the freight cost of merchandise delivered to the store. Because freight "in" is considered a part of the cost of the merchandise, I have posted it to that account.

Other Expenses

The second item we have on our distribution sheet is *advertising*. The next account is *telephone*, which is usually a once-a-month posting. The next is *utilities*. This includes both natural gas/electric and water/garbage. The telephone posting could also be made to this account, except that most operators want to keep it separate. This is so that they can have the figure at their fingertips without digging it out of an accumulative figure. This, naturally, is for control and administrative purposes.

Next, we have *truck (auto) expense.* This usually consists of the cost of gasoline, oil changes, tires, and other such items. If the shop has no other equipment, then equipment repair would also be posted to this auto or truck expense. It might be a good point to mention the fact that the Internal Revenue frowns upon total deductible expense for store vehicles unless they are actually used totally for business purposes. If the vehicle is driven home at night or used on weekends for pleasure driving, they might dispute some of the expenses for it.

The next account is the *rent account.* I have already explained the *draw.* Notice how it is handled in the check distribution. Any amount of money that is taken for personal use, from an ice cream cone to the cost of a new swimming pool, must be posted to the drawing account. It is NOT necessary to explain what the money is for; only the fact that it was withdrawn for the owner's personal expenses. It is the owner's money and as much as is needed can be withdrawn, unless the owner begins to overdraw the value of his or her *net worth* (equity in the business). I will repeat that this is not the amount on which the proprietor pays income tax. This tax is based on the *net profit,* not withdrawals from the business.

Other Accounts

The last column, *other accounts,* contains items which happen so infrequently that it wouldn't be worthwhile to have a separate column for them. Some of these items, like the loan payment, happen once a month, while others occur less frequently. In order to keep from having a distribution sheet six feet wide, it is better to post these seldom-used items in the other accounts column. Write in what they are for and post them to the appropriate accounts or columns when the time comes.

I have posted the truck payment to this other accounts column. Since this is one of the most misunderstood postings, I should explain why this amount ($25.00) is not posted as an expense in the "truck expense" column. Certainly, it is payment for the truck and the truck is an expense of the company.

Wrong!

The truck is an investment. Only the *operation of the truck* is classified as an expense to the business.

When Hazel went into business, she needed capital with which to open her shop. Regardless of how small her shop might be or how restrained her services might be, cash must be put up for the purchase of merchandise, payment of rent, starting utilities services, installing a telephone, buying a truck, and so forth.

Since she was starting on a shoestring, Hazel didn't have enough money to do all of these things. She went to the bank and borrowed some money. When combined with her own initial cash, this gave her enough to purchase the fixtures, pay a month's rent for the shop, install a phone, and so forth. So what she is now paying when she writes the $25.00 check for the truck, or the $35.00 a week for the fixtures, is money she borrowed to put with her capital so that she would have enough.

The salesperson had Hazel sign a contract. The used-car lot then got their money from Hazel's bank. But it was Hazel's loan which she used to make a *capital purchase.* The value of the truck goes into her assets under the heading of "Equipment—Truck," and the payments are shown as a payment on her loan. *The only way Hazel can expense any portion of the value of her truck is through depreciation.* This allows the owner to get back the value of the truck, by deducting the major portion of the total value in little bits from profits. This is achieved through the means of expensing depreciation each month.

Depreciation

How depreciation will be calculated depends on when the property was acquired. If you acquired the property between 1981 and 1986, the Accelerated Cost Recovery System (ACRS) created by the Economic Recovery Tax Act of 1981 is used. Property acquired after 1986 is depreciated under the Modified Accelerated Cost Recovery System (MACRS) created by the Tax Reform Act of 1986.

Since Hazel's is a used "light duty" truck and was purchased after 1986, we can figure depreciation over a five-year life expectancy period. (Your local IRS office can offer additional information as to life expectancy for other types of property.) Under ACRS Hazel would get to use a three-year depreciation period. MACRS provides for a 200 percent declining balance method of depreciation with a switch to the straight-line method after a few years. The exact depreciation depends on which quarter of the year the property was acquired. We'll assume that Hazel bought the truck in the first quarter. That would allow Hazel to deduct 25 percent of the cost the first year, 21.43 percent the second year, 15.31 percent the third year, 10.93 percent the fourth year, 8.75 percent the fifth year, 8.74 percent the sixth year and 1.09 percent in the seventh and final year. (These figures are available in tables published by the IRS.) For the current (first) year, we take the total cost of the truck, $2,500.00, and determine our depreciation for the first year as $625.00 We can then divide this amount by twelve to get a monthly depreciation expense of $52.08. Under the ACRS system, Hazel would be allowed first-year depreciation of 25 percent of the cost, followed by 38% the second year, and 37 percent for the third and final year. Under this method the depreciation for the first year would be $244.21, and the monthly depreciation expense would be $20.35.

In expensing this amount, we post that figure to our "depreciation expense" account in the "operating expense" section of the general ledger (Figure 18). The same figure is also posted to another account called the "reserve for depreciation." This is an account in the asset section of the financial statement (and general ledger) which immediately follows the account "equipment—truck" in the next space below (Figure 15).

The original purchase price of the truck always remains the same in the asset section until it is removed from the business. The depreciation accumulates month by month until it reaches the original purchase price. These figures stay on the financial statement, and in the books, until the unit is either sold, junked, or traded on a new piece of equipment.

We will go into the actual posting of depreciation in Chapter 7. Note that the check distribution, a double entry record of paid-outs, can be expanded to cover any accounts that might be added to the business as it grows.

The Service Business

There are several types of businesses that sell a service rather than a product. These still need a system of record keeping. These records will show the owner how much income is generated, and how much net profit will be left at the end of the year.

This group includes such people as accountants, engineers, architects, lawyers, doctors, and dentists. In addition, a cleaning

Figure 13

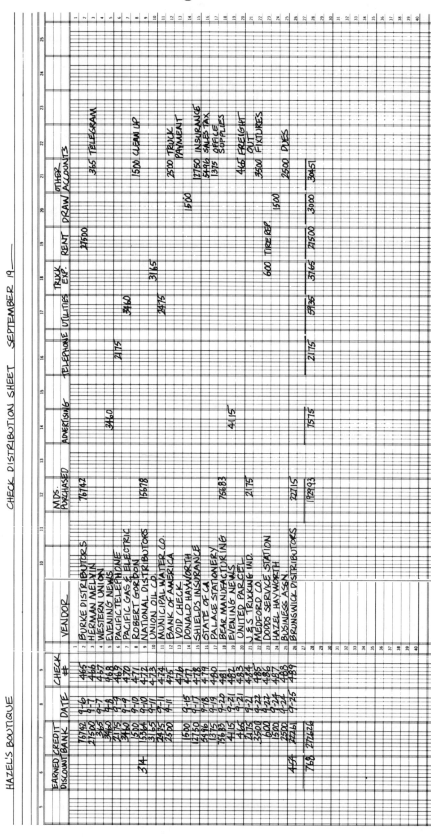

establishment, a beauty parlor, an advertising agency, a shopping service, or a free-lance writer would also be classified in such a category. These types of businesses dispense nothing but a service for which they receive a fee (unless they sell a bottle of hair tonic or a comb, as could be the case of the beauty parlor). The doctor charges a set fee for treating a patient in the office. An accountant might charge a monthly fee for the amount of time spent accomplishing the task. The dentist might charge a set fee for each tooth pulled, another for a tooth filled, and still another for making up a set of dentures. However, most of the professional's earnings come from fees for services rather than from a product he/she has for sale.

In order to keep track of the income due the professional, it is necessary for the bookkeeper or accountant to keep a service card on each patient/client. This card shows what the service was, and the amount of money the client/patient owes. When payment for the service is received, it is also posted to the client's card.

Such a record might look a little like the following:

Doctor Martin J. Astro
1495 No. Mission Street
Capitola, California
426-9879

Patient: Arthur P. Douglass
             1312 North Main Street
             Soquel, CA 95073   September 23, 19____

Date	Description	Debits	Credits	Balance
9-3-75	Office visit	$20.00		$20.00
9-7-75	Office visit	15.00		35.00
9-12-75	Office visit	10.00		45.00
9-21-75	R.O.A. Ck #214		$45.00	-0-

As payments are received, they are posted to the "cash received" sheet for the day. Such a sheet might appear somewhat like our posting for merchandise sold, including taxes. It should be a very simple posting. Perhaps it will look somewhat like the example in Figure 10.

In looking over this sheet, please bear in mind that if there should be any kind of product sold, it would be necessary to break down the sales between fees and sales. The tax would then be shown on the "cash-received" sheet. Normally, this is not done by a professional person, as they usually hire a bookkeeper or bookkeeping service from their very first day of business. If you are setting up an office on a shoestring, however, this is the best way to handle your daily records.

Figure 14

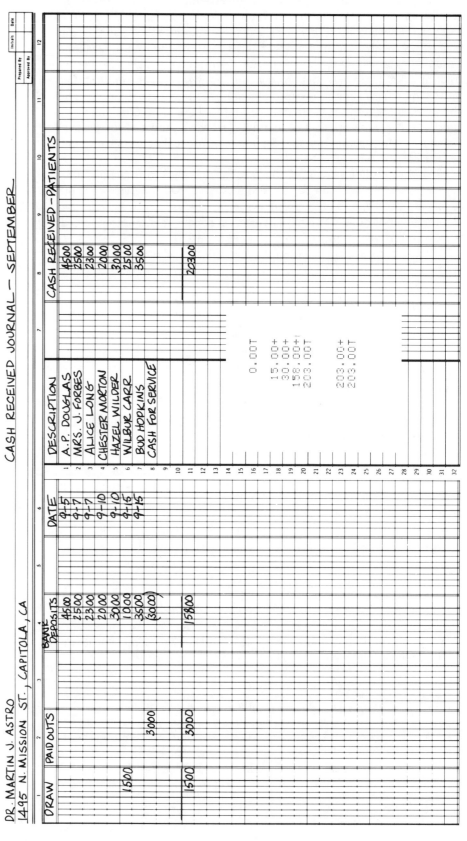

5

Posting to the General Ledger from the Cash and Sales Journal

In setting up a new accounting system, one of the first things the accountant does is to determine the various accounts the client will need in posting the books. Every business does not use the same accounts, nor does it need them. The accounts used by a heating contractor could be markedly different from the accounts used by the small shop owner. Which accounts will be used by the owner and will appear on the "Chart of Accounts" will have to be determined by the owner.

A good test of the number and the names of the accounts an owner will choose would be to ask himself a question: What do I want my records to tell me which will help me make significant decisions about operating my business tomorrow, the next day, next week, next month, five years from now? Ignoring for a moment the requirements of various regulatory authorities, the basic purpose of all record keeping is to provide the means of submitting information to owners to assist them in making these meaningful decisions about the future.

Chart of Accounts

Breaking the operating costs down into the various items that are usually shown is for the benefit of the owner (and the Internal Revenue Service). These show which portions of the operating expenses are taking the most money. The operating expenses are usually referred to as the "controllable accounts" in comparing them to the "merchandise purchased" and "cost of sales" accounts. It is only over these operating expenses that the owner can exercise some form of control. (Naturally a cheaper grade of merchandise can be stocked, and a cheaper freight carrier can be used. But this might only result in decreasing sales volume or sales prices. So it is conceded that in order to maintain a quality merchandise, the owner must pay the price.)

It is only rent, advertising, telephone and utility expenses that can be kept under the owner's control. He/she can rent a cheaper place for the shop, or advertise less often, or use a less expensive phone set-up. It is up to the owner or operator to determine the options that exist and increase or decrease the account spending which does the most good for the business.

In setting up a Chart of Accounts for Hazel's Boutique, we have taken the income statement as presented before. Added to it are the assets and liabilities that we dreamed up for her financial statement. In looking forward to the needs of a complete double entry accounting system, the reserves for depreciation were also added. There is only one item left out at this point. This is a Reserve for Bad Debts. Since the small business owner does not, by economic necessity, carry many charge accounts, it is not applicable at this point.

(Bad debts are handled in the same fashion as depreciation, in that a Reserve for Bad Debts is set up. Whenever a charge customer goes sour and collection isn't possible, then the amount is posted to the Reserve for Bad Debts. It is a credit figure in the asset section following Accounts Receivable. This same amount is posted to an expense account called "Bad Debt Expense." The amount *stays in the accounts receivable until it is proven that it will never be collected. It is then taken from the accounts receivable amount and out of the reserve.* If the sale has not been counted as a sale and entered into the total sales, *it cannot be written off as a bad debt.* It cannot be counted as bad if it has never been entered as a sale.)

The Chart of Accounts that follows is as it might appear in Hazel's boutique.

Hazel Hayworth
DBA Hazel's Boutique
921 Haywood Drive
Santa Cruz, California

Chart of Accounts

Assets

Cash in bank
Accounts Receivable
Reserve for Bad Debts
Inventory
Prepaid Expenses (Rent, insurance, etc.)
Deposits (Sales tax, telephone, etc.)
Equipment—Truck
Reserve for Depreciation
Furniture and Fixtures
Reserve for Depreciation
Office Equipment
Reserve for Depreciation
Leasehold Improvements (Additions to leased property)
Reserve for Amortization

Liabilities

Accounts Payable
Loans Payable
- Truck
- Fixtures
- Office Equipment
Taxes Payable—Personal Property
Taxes Payable—Sales Tax
Taxes Payable—Payroll Taxes

Capital

Hazel Hayworth Investment
Hazel Hayworth Drawing Account

Income

Income
Leather Goods
Apparel
Footwear—Shoes
Jewelry
Toys

Cost of Sales

Merchandise Purchased
Freight In
Payroll

Operating Expense

Rent
Advertising Expense
Telephone Expense
Utilities Expense

Insurance Expense
Truck or Auto Expense
Accounting or Legal Services
    Expense
Office Expense
Depreciation Expense
Payroll Tax Expense
Taxes & License (Business
    license, business taxes, truck
    license)
Interest Expense
Over/Short Expense
Dues, Subscriptions,
    Contributions
(Discounts Earned)
(Other Income)
Miscellaneous Expense

We now have a cash and sales journal and a check distribution sheet. We should post the figures from these to our flatform ledger. Posting to the same one we used before (only another copy), and adding the new items we have explored (the assets, the liabilities, and the new month of September), we come up with a new balance sheet and income statement.

Take a look now at the new flatform ledger and you will see that it gives a great deal more information than did Romulus' simple sheet, or the first accumulative sheets we made up for Hazel. Figures 15, 16, 17, and 18 are the new ledger (Chapter 6).

In order to save confusion after the flatform ledger is posted and you are prepared to calculate a total amount of net profit, I suggest that all credit figures be bracketed on the ledger. This way, all normal figures would go as a plus figure into your adding machine, and all bracketed figures would be minus figures in your machine.

By having credit figures bracketed on the flatform ledger, you can tell at a glance they are different from normal figures. There might be a time when the bracketed figure will be added and the normal figure will be subtracted, depending on what is happening in your business. Only your own knowledge and experience will tell you when this will happen.

We will begin our posting with the cash and sales journal and post the first item of the sales breakdown which is "Apparel." The total of the item column is $3,633.23. Post this amount to the apparel line of our flatform ledger in the September columns. Then we can tick off the figure on the sales sheet with a red pencil. This way, anyone looking at it will know that it has been posted. Then go on to the next sales item, which is "Leather Goods." The amount of leather goods is $1,719.29. Post this figure to the leather goods line on the ledger sheet. Follow through with the rest of the sales, then post the accounts receivable total of $475.21. This figure represents the amount due the business from extending credit to charge customers and is the amount we will bill them at the end of the month.

Post the $475.21 without brackets in the column, **Cash Rec. (Sales)** on the Accounts Receivable line on the flatform ledger.

The next column in the cash and sales journal is headed **Cash** and it is shown under **Sales**. It represents the amount of sales which were sold for cash during the month. This figure will not be posted anywhere since it is merely a balancing amount to arrive at total cash taken in during the month. For now, skip past this amount and we will return later to see how it is involved in the proving process.

The next two columns to the right are the sales taxes added to the charge customers' sales for the month and the actual sales taxes collected in cash. The purpose of segregating the sales tax from charge sales and sales tax from cash sales is to help us prove the total **Cash In** figure shown on the cash and sales journal. When we post the sales tax to our flatform ledger, however, we will combine the two sales tax figures and post their sum, $380.63, in brackets. You see, the tax due the state is a total liability of the business, and it does not matter to the state authority how much was collected from charge and from cash customers. They want only the total we collected and will collect when our charge customers pay us. As a side issue, even if one or more of our charge customers fails to pay the total balance due us, our business is still responsible for payment of the sales tax.

In the next column, **Paid on Account**, $115.35 is the total cash our charge customers have paid us on the bills due. Since September is the first month we have extended credit, this amount must be what charge customers have paid against the amounts they charged this month. The amount will be posted in the column **Cash Rec. (Sales)** in brackets on the flatform ledger, and it will be deducted from the $475.21 which we charged to customers this month to arrive at the balance still due the business at month's end. Of course, if there had been a balance owing at the beginning of September, the difference between the charges and the payments would be added (greater charges) or deducted (greater payments) to that beginning balance.

The next columns are headed **Other Cash—Account** and **Amount**. These columns provide the means to record additions to cash which are of a nature other than sales or payments on account. Loans, additions to capital, sales of assets are some of the types of entries properly included under this heading. In September, Hazel's Boutique borrowed $1,000 from a bank for working capital purposes. You will want to post this amount in brackets in the column **Cash Rec. (Sales)** on the **Loans Payable** line under the liability section on your flatform ledger. It represents the amount which the business is responsible for paying back to the bank when the note comes due.

The column within the two double lines, **Total Cash In**, is a proofing figure and will not be posted anywhere. To show how it is derived, we can arrive at it and then prove it. Starting with the **Sales** amounts at the far left columns, add $3,633.23, $1,719.29, $636.02, and $382.12, which total $6,370.66, the grand sum of sales for the month of September. As you know, some of these are charge sales and do not represent cash at the moment of sale. The column **Sales—Accounts Receivable** has a total of $475.21 and it is the sum of $448.31 in actual sales and $26.90 in sales tax. (Other than totaling the sale slips for charges, one quick way of determining the sales figure from the $475.21 is to divide the $475.21 by

1.06, assuming that sales are 100% and the sales tax is 6%.) Deducting $448.31 of charge sales from the total of $6,370.66 we find the aggregate of cash sales is $5,922.35, and this is a cash taken in figure. So, to arrive at the **Total Cash In** figure, we will add $5,922.35 for cash sales, $353.73 for sales tax collected on cash sales, the $115.35 collected on charge accounts, and the $1,000.00 loan proceeds from the bank. Total of all is $7,391.42. Let's prove that figure.

Total of all sales is $6,370.66, including charge sales. To this amount, add both charge and sales taxes, $380.63; the collections on account, $115.35; and the bank loan, $1,000.00 and the value is $7,866.64. From this amount, we deduct the charges to customers' accounts, $475.21 (these are non-cash items for this month), and we prove the $7,391.43 for **Total Cash In**. As you now know, this total is a proofing figure and is not posted anywhere.

Moving along to the right, it is time to post Hazel's draw of $125.00 during September. On the flatform ledger under the **Capital** section, you will find the account, **Hazel Hayworth, Drawing**. Under the column **Cash Rec.—Sales**, post the $125.00 without brackets. Don't be upset when you recognize that the draw is not a cash receipt for the business; to the contrary, it is a cash **Pay Out**. The heading of the column is a bit deceptive, but it allows us to record a *reduction* to Hazel's capital by *increasing* her drawing account. This makes sense when we realize that the boutique *owes* Hazel the money she originally invested *and* the profits the business generates as time goes by. Obviously, any amount which Hazel draws from time to time *decreases* the amount the business *owes* her at the time of drawing.

The next column is a total of all the pay outs for whatever purpose other than Hazel's draw. On the reverse side of the journal (not shown), we would have previously written a description of the purposes for each pay out. The $16.20 was paid for incidental clean up by a local high school student. This is a relatively minor amount and will probably not be repeated in the near future, so we can label it as a **Miscellaneous Expense**. As such, it will be posted under the **Operating Expenses** section, on the **Misc. Expenses** line, under the column **Cash Rec.—Sales**. Here, too, you should show no concern about the columnar heading because of the explanation in the preceding paragraph. The next amount we post is $150.00. The reverse side of the journal notes it is an amount spent for merchandise purchased in the apparel line. Post this amount under the **Cost of Sales** section, on the **Merchandise Purchased** line, under the **Cash Rec.—Sales** column. The last amount of cash paid out is $22.10 and is for postage stamps and envelopes. We can consider the amount as part of office expense. Under the **Operating Expenses** section, on the **Office Expense** line, under the **Cash Rec.—Sales** column, we will post this amount.

The next column to the right indicates a cash overage of $1.84. It is reasonable to believe the handling of cash during the course of a month will occasionally result in small, acceptable errors. This figure is the net of those errors and will be posted under the **Operating Expenses** section on the **(Over)/Short** line. We will want to put brackets around the posting under the column **Cash Rec.—Sales** because this overage is not an expense of the business but a *reduction* to the expense of operating. Most owners review this overage/shortage account to see that the amounts remain acceptably small. Too many overages could mean clerks are shortchanging customers. Continuing businesses cannot long tolerate that.

The next column, **Total—Cash Paid Out,** is also a proofing figure and not to be posted anywhere. It is the total of the preceding three columns to the left. When it is deducted from the **Total Cash In** column, it shows the amount of money which should have been deposited into the bank for that day's, that month's activity. Most business owners do not use night depository for the end of the month's business deposits. If you do not (or if you do but your bank does not record one night's deposits until the next banking day), then obviously, the last day's deposits will not appear on your bank statement until the following month. Nonetheless, each month's business must be clearly identified and your bank reconcilement will reflect the last day's deposit as a deposit in transit.

The total of cash deposited (or depositable) for September, $7,079.97, will be posted without brackets under the **Assets** section on the **Cash In Bank** line under the column **Cash Rec.—Sales**. This act completes posting from the cash and sales journal.

Now that you understand the workings of this system, we can get on to bigger and better things. We will now post the double entry paid out check distribution journal.

6

Posting to the General Ledger from the Double Entry Check Register

From the check register, Figure 13, we will post the September figures in our flatform ledger, represented by Figures 15-18. While looking over this month's posting, you will notice that I have a column headed "Paid Outs Etc." All figures from the September check distribution sheet will be posted to this column. (We posted the cash and sales journal to the "Cash Received—Sales" column.)

In preparing to post from our check distribution (paid out sheet) to our flatform ledger, I am assuming that it has been added up and the totals checked across the bottom so that we will be certain it is in balance.

The first column to study is merchandise purchased. You will notice that it covers total purchased and is not broken down according to the type of merchandise purchased. We may study the breakdown later, but right now it is not necessary. So, let us post the columns.

First we will post:

Merchandise purchased	$1,929.93
Advertising	75.75
Telephone Expense	21.75
Utilities	59.35
Truck Expense	37.65
Rent Expense	275.00
Hazel Hayworth Drawing	30.00

Our last column is another of the other account columns which usually gets the leftovers which have no other place to go. I have recapped this column below.

September Check Distribution

Loan Truck—$25.00	$ 25.00
Loan Fixtures—$35.00	35.00

Sales Tax—$54.96	54.96
Insurance—$127.50	127.50
Office—$13.75	13.75
Dues and Cont.—$25.00	25.00
Miscellaneous—$3.65/$15.00/$4.65	23.30
	$304.51

This completes our unbracketed debit entries. We have only the two credit columns to post in order to finish, both of which will appear in brackets. These two columns are the **Credit To Bank** column (showing the amount of checks written or the amount taken from the bank account through the means of checks) and the **Discounts Earned** column. After you examine these postings on the ledger sheets, we will prove all September postings and then make up an Income Statement from the information now available.

Up to this point we are dealing with September's figures only. It is good to see later how the business prospered for September, but we are also interested in knowing how the business fared for the period year-to-date, including September and all the prior months. To determine cumulative figures, we will need to combine September's activity with prior months.

Before we can combine this month's postings and arrive at cumulative account balances, we should prove that all postings under each columnar heading have the proper amounts as shown in the cash and sales journal and check distribution journal. We do this by entering into an adding machine all bracketed items as minuses and all unbracketed items as plusses. If the resultant total is zero, it means the amounts transferred from each journal sheet are accurate and you have done a good job. To illustrate, start with the **Cash Rec.—Sales** column and enter into your adding machine the following: **Cash In Bank**, +7,079.97; **Accounts Receivable**, −115.35, +475.21; **Loans Payable—Bank**, −1,000.00; **Taxes Payable (Sales Tax)**, −380.63; **Hazel Hayworth Drawing**, +125.00; **Income—Leather Goods**, −1,719.29, **Apparel**, −3,633.23, **Shoes**, −382.12, ᴊewelry, −636.02, **Merchandise Purchased**, +150.00; **Office Expense**, +22.10, **(Over)/Short**, −1.84; and **Misc. Expense**, +16.20. If you have followed carefully, your adding machine total should now be zero. Following the same procedure for the **Paid Outs (Ck. Distr.)** column must produce the same zero result. Time now to combine September's figures to arrive at cumulative year-to-date totals.

The interesting aspect of my construction of the flatform ledger is the capability of producing both a monthly Income Statement and a statement showing income for year to date. Obviously, both sets of figures are desirable in business analysis.

Once you have established a zero footing of each of September's columns, your next step is to extend (meaning to arrive at the difference between the postings in the **Cash Rec.** column and those in the **Paid Out** column) the balances of each account into the column **Total for Month**. As before, zero foot this column to prove. It is from this source, as you will see later, that you will pick up the information to construct financial statements for the month of September.

Figure 15

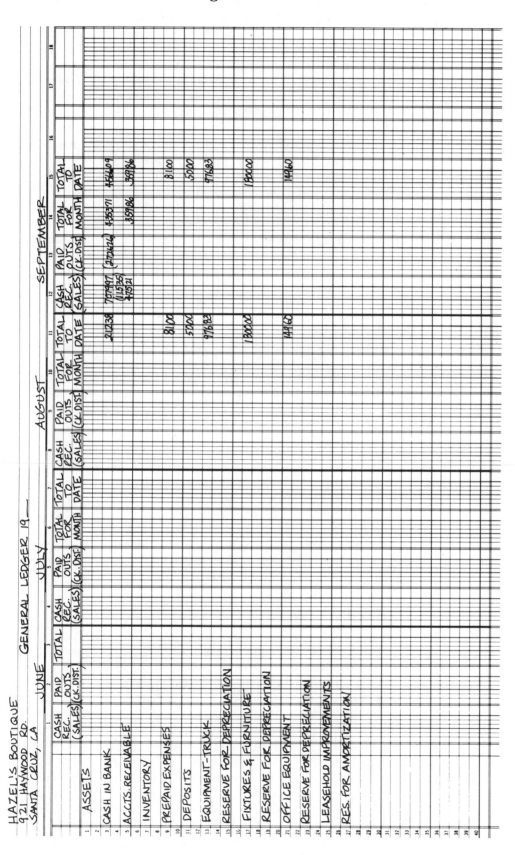

Following that task, the next and final step is to extend **Total For Month** figures into the column **Total to Date.** Not difficult to do. Starting with each account beginning with those in the **Assets** section, refer to the balance in the account shown in the column **Total to Date** under August. If that balance is bracketed, enter it into your adding machine as a minus. Refer to the balance in the column **Total for Month** under September. If it is bracketed, enter it into your adding machine as a minus. Arrive at a total of the two sums and enter it in the column **Total to Date** under September. If either balance, August's or September's, is unbracketed, you will enter that balance in your adding machine as a plus. Once again, zero foot to prove your extensions.

Looking over the ledger sheets, we find that most of the same information is available which would be found in an accrual accounting system. We have worked up the sales and check distribution accounts for the months-to-date. We also have a record of the drawing of money from the business by the owner. We should be able to make up a preliminary Income Statement and balance sheet by using this new information.

What is Missing

Except. . . . .

In order to keep the income and financial records accurate, we must know how much money is owed to suppliers of merchandise received but for which we have not yet paid. We arrive at this figure by adding up all the unpaid invoices. All that is needed is a total figure. Do not enter the figure on the ledger sheet, but save it to use on our Income Statement.

What is Needed For the Income Statement

In preparing our Income Statement, we must have an inventory figure for the end of September. We will assume that Hazel has had a physical inventory count and has come up with $162.75. This is not much of an inventory, but we can assume that Hazel is having a sale on seasonal merchandise which would explain the large sales and small purchase amounts for our accounting period. Again, these figures are arbitrary and do not represent an actual business.

Cost of Merchandise Sold

Our first need in preparing our Income Statement (profit and loss statement) is an actual cost of the merchandise sold. With this information, we can come up with a realistic gross profit figure. Cost of merchandise sold is calculated by using three pieces of information: beginning inventory, merchandise purchased, and ending inventory. Refer to Figure 19, Exhibit 1, Cost of Sales, where you'll see that operating figures are given both for the month of September and for the year to date.

Since this is a new store, we assume the beginning inventory is zero. We enter zero on our work sheet after a heading of "Inventory— Beginning June 1, 19____." This was the month the store opened for business. Next we will write in the amount of merchandise purchased

Figure 16

HAZEL'S BOUTIQUE   GENERAL LEDGER

HAZEL'S BOUTIQUE — GENERAL LEDGER

	JUNE			JULY				AUGUST				SEPTEMBER			
	CASH REC. (SALES)	PAID OUTS (CK.DIST)	TOTAL	CASH REC. (SALES)	PAID OUTS (CK.DIST)	TOTAL FOR MONTH	TOTAL TO DATE	CASH REC. (SALES)	PAID OUTS (CK.DIST)	TOTAL FOR MONTH	TOTAL TO DATE	CASH REC. (SALES)	PAID OUTS (CK.DIST)	TOTAL FOR MONTH	TOTAL TO DATE
INCOME															
LEATHER GOODS	47595		47595	51920		51920	99515	46161		46161	267159	(171929)		(171929)	(454088)
APPAREL	37322		37322	257137		25737	63059	15377		15377	78436	(363323)		(363323)	341159
SHOES	29586		29586	15607		15607	45193				45193	(38212)		(38212)	(834.05)
JEWELRY	27319		27319	9975		9975	37294	18908		18908	66102	(63602)		(63602)	(117104)
COST OF SALES															
MERCHANDISE PURCHASE		78005	78005		56781	56781	134786	2723	41565	44288	179074	15000	192993	207993	387067
FREIGHT IN		2660	2660		1793	1793	4453		1260	1260	5713				5713
PAYROLL															
TOTAL COST OF SALES			80665			58574	139239			45548	184787				
OPERATING EXPENSES															
RENT		8900	8900		8900	8900	17800		8900	8900	26700		17500	17500	44200
ADVERTISING		1723	1723		1690	1690	3413		1975	1975	5388		7575	7575	12963
TELEPHONE		1563	1563		1415	1415	2978		763	763	3741		2175	2175	5916
UTILITIES		1923	1923		1850	1850	3773		1742	1742	5515		5935	5935	11450

Figure 18

HAZEL'S BOUTIQUE GENERAL LEDGER 19__

OPERATING EXPENSES—(CONTINUED)	JUNE CASH REC. (SALES)	JUNE PAID OUTS (CK. DIST.)	JUNE TOTAL	JULY CASH REC. (SALES)	JULY PAID OUTS (CK. DIST.)	JULY TOTAL FOR MONTH	JULY TOTAL TO DATE	AUGUST CASH REC. (SALES)	AUGUST PAID OUTS (CK. DIST.)	AUGUST TOTAL FOR MONTH	AUGUST TOTAL TO DATE	SEPTEMBER CASH REC. (SALES)	SEPTEMBER PAID OUTS (CK. DIST.)	SEPTEMBER TOTAL FOR MONTH	SEPTEMBER TOTAL TO DATE
INSURANCE EXP.		125 00	125 00				125 00				125 00		127 50	127 50	252 50
TRUCK OR AUTO		27 50	27 50		19 20	19 20	46 70		29 17	29 17	75 87		37 65	37 65	113 52
ACCOUNTING OR LEGAL					10 00	10 00	10 00				10 00				10 00
OFFICE EXP.		3 50	3 50				3 50		12 30	12 30	15 80	22 10	13 75	35 85	51 65
DEPRECIATION															
PAYROLL TAX															
TAXES & LICENSE		17 50	17 50				17 50				17 50				17 50
INTEREST															
(OVER)/SHORT								20		20	20	(1 84)		(1 84)	(1 64)
DUES, CONTRIBUTIONS, SUBSCRIPTIONS													25 00	25 00	25 00
(DISCOUNTS EARNED)													(7 68)	(7 68)	(7 68)
(OTHER INCOME)															
MISC. EXP.		9 20	9 20				9 20		8 60	8 60	17 80	16 20	23 30	39 50	57 30

for the month of September and for the year to date. These figures are taken from the Cost of Sales section of the flatform ledger (Figure 17). The total of the checks written to pay for merchandise to sell was $2,079.93 for September and $3,870.67 for year to date. To this we will add the amount of "freight in" which must be classified as part of the merchandise cost. These two figures give us total purchased as entered on our check distribution sheet. It was also posted to the merchandise purchased account on our flatform ledger. **But it does not include invoices not paid.** To these totals we will add **the amount of our accounts payable, the total of invoices for merchandise purchased and possibly sold but not yet paid for.** *This is the operation which turns our double entry cash method of accounting for taxes into an accrual method of accounting for taxes. This gives the owner a realistic picture of the cost of sales.*

This figure is not placed in the ledger but is used at this point only for calculation purposes. Each time a statement is made up, we take figures from the ledger which do not contain the payables.

In the following month, when the checks are written to pay for more merchandise, this amount will be paid along with others. It will then be entered in the check distribution sheet. By using only the amounts paid on the ledger and adding in the "not paid" only when making up a statement, we have an accurate bookkeeping system which affords less possibility of error. This is what accounting is all about when it comes to the new small business. If the cost of sales is actual, the net profit will be actual. This is the simplest method of accounting. It also saves a lot of work.

The Value of Merchandise

So now, by adding the payables to our total paid purchases, we have new purchase figures of $3,055.38 for September and $4,903.25 for year to date. This is the amount of merchandise brought into the store to be sold during our period of accounting (June through September). Since there was no beginning inventory, these figures represent merchandise in the store available for sale. Since we have a small ending inventory value of $162.75 which was taken at the end of our accounting period, we place it on our work sheet and subtract it from the total available for sale. This gives balances of $2,892.63 for September and $4,740.50 for year to date, which is the value or cost of the merchandise sold during the months for which we are accounting. We will now mark the work sheet as Exhibit 1, Cost of Sales and will use this figure as the cost of merchandise sold on our Income Statement.

The construction of the Income Statement, which represents operating figures for September and for the year to date, is accomplished by transferring figures from the flatform ledger to the Income Statement. By referring to both the flatform ledger (Figures 15-18) and the Income Statement (Figure 20), you can see how this was done.

Our completed Income Statement shows a realistic net profit for the volume of business transacted. Now we can prepare the Balance Sheet.

The Balance Sheet is usually set up in the same manner as the example of the flatform ledger given previously. This is so unless the assets and liabilities cover so many items as to require an entire sheet of paper. In such a case, they would be typed on separate sheets and placed in a folder so that they would open out like a book to display both pages at the same time.

At this stage, we might repeat that everything the business owns, it also owes to both outsiders and those who own the business. Romulus, our slave, conducted his business in such a fashion that he knew how much belonged to his master and how much belonged to suppliers. Our Balance Sheet gives the same information.

Every dollar taken in and placed in the bank must be parceled out to someone or something. If suddenly turned into cash, the value of the inventory, the equipment, the furniture and fixtures, the office equipment and supplies would have to be paid out. It would go to the bank for loans, or the distributors for merchandise purchased, to the state and federal government for taxes owed, and finally, to the owner. The owner's portion would equal the amount of "equity" or the net worth of the business. This manner of keeping books is still the same as when Romulus made up his own first Income Statement and Balance Sheet.

Preparing the Balance Sheet

Figures are placed on the Balance Sheet in order of their liquidity. This means the order in which they can be converted into cash. Obviously, the most liquid asset of all is cash. Our amount is $4,566.09. Next in liquidity is accounts receivable and this amount is $359.86. You can trace how this balance came to be by subtracting payments on account from the amounts charged to customers on account. The next item is the inventory figure of $162.75 which was supplied by Hazel from her actual physical inventory.

Deposits of $50. appear next and then they lead into the items of a fixed asset (longer life than current period) nature. These fixed assets are the truck, furniture and fixtures, and the office equipment. Prepaid expenses, that is, those expenses which have been paid in advance and will be used in the business in later accounting periods, always appear last on the asset side of the balance sheet. These items have a value only insofar as they will be used up. Rarely is there a redemption value attached to them in cash equivalency.

Totaling the assets, we find the business owns $8,146.13 in assigned values. Later you will see this total is not accurate because depreciation must be deducted from the carrying values of the various types of equipment.

Remembering that a business owes to outsiders and insiders everything it owns, we now turn to the liability (outsiders) and capital/proprietorship (insiders) section. Again according to liquidity, we find accounts payable as the first amount the business must pay off in cash. While the taxing authority could take issue with the concept (they want to believe their sales taxes, etc. will be subject to earlier payoff than general creditors), it is usual to see accounts payable shown before other payables.

Items to Appear on the Balance Sheet

Following accounts payable are sales taxes payable of $380.63 and the various loans payable totaling $2,040.00. When all these figures are combined, the total liabilities of the boutique are $3,396.08. Another way to look at the significance of this sum is to realize that $3,396.08 of all the $8,146.13 assets must be satisfied before the owner can expect to reap any of the harvested earnings at the date of the Balance Sheet.

The last portion of this financial statement indicates what the business owes to the owner through capital. It is good to show the history of the proprietorship by showing any investment by the owner since the last statement was prepared. In this case we have a first statement, so the investment shown is the original one by Hazel. To that sum we add the profit, year to date, and we deduct the owner's drawings for the same period. You can see that Hazel's initial investment of $753.43 has grown to $4,750.05

If this statement represented a full year's activities, then the $4,750.05 of proprietorship would appear on the line, **Hazel Hayworth, Investment** in the next statement prepared.

Finally, we add the proprietorship total to the liabilities total. Since this total equals that of the assets, our sheet is in balance.

An Income Statement and Balance Sheet have now been produced which used information drawn from figures accumulated by our cash method of accounting for taxes. I think it looks rather good. It is accurate to the extent that the net profit is accurate. This is really the name of the game at this particular point.

Figure 19

Hazel Hayworth T/A Hazel's Boutique
Exhibit 1—Cost of Sales
as of Sept. 30, 19____

	Month of Sept. 19____	Year to Date Sept. 30, 19____
Inventory, Beginning		
June 1, 19____	$ —0—	$ —0—
Add:		
Merchandise Purchased	$2,079.93	$3,870.67
Freight In	$ —0—	57.13
Total Entered Purchases	$2,079.93	$3,927.80
Merchandise Not Entered	975.45	975.45
(Unpaid Invoices)		
Total Merchandise		
Purchased	$3,055.38	$4,093.25
Merchandise Available		
for Sale	$3,055.38	$4,093.25
Less:		
Inventory, Ending		
Sept. 30	162.75	162.75
Cost of Sales	$2,892.63	$4740.50

Figure 20

Hazel Hayworth T/A Hazel's Boutique
Income Statement for the Month of September and
Year-to-Date Ending September 30, 19___

	Month of Sept. 19___	Year to Date Sept. 30, 19___
Income from Sales:		
Leather Goods	$1,719.29	$4,346.88
Apparel	3,633.23	4,417.59
Shoes	382.12	834.05
Jewelry	636.02	1,197.04
Total Sales	$6,370.66	$10,795.56
Less: Cost of Sales	2,892.63	4,740.50
(Exhibit 1)		
Gross Profit on Sales:	$3,478.03	$ 6,055.06
Operating Expenses:		
Rent	$ 275.00	$ 542.00
Advertising	75.75	129.63
Telephone	21.75	59.16
Utilities	59.35	114.50
Insurance	127.50	252.50
Truck or Auto	37.65	113.52
Accounting or Legal	—0—	10.00
Office	35.85	51.65
Taxes and Licenses	—0—	17.50
(Over)/Short	(1.84)	(1.64)
Dues, Contributions	25.00	25.00
Discounts Earned	(7.68)	(7.68)
Miscellaneous	39.50	57.30
Total Operating Expense	$ 687.83	$ 1,363.44
Net Profit for the Periods	$2,790.20	$ 4,691.62

Figure 21

Hazel Hayworth T/A Hazel's Boutique
Balance Sheet as of September 30, 19____

Assets:

Cash on Hand and in Bank	$4,566.09	
Accounts Receivable	359.86	
Inventory	162.75	
Deposits	50.00	
Equipment-Truck	976.83	
Furniture and Fixtures	1,800.00	
Office Equipment	149.00	
Prepaid Expenses	81.00	
Total Assets		$8,146.13

Liabilities and Proprietorship:

Liabilities

Accounts Payable		$ 975.45	
Sales Taxes Payable		380.63	
Loans Payable:			
Truck	$ 275.00		
Fixtures	765.00		
Bank	1,000.00	$2,040.00	
Total Liabilities			$3,396.08

Proprietorship

Hazel Hayworth, Investment		$ 753.43	
Profit, Year-to-Date		4,691.62	
		$5,445.05	
Less: Draw, Year-to-Date		695.00	
Total Proprietorship			4,750.05
Total Liabilities and			
Proprietorship			$8,146.13

In spite of the fact that our Income Statement shows a net profit of $4,691.62 for the period of time that the store has been doing business, this does not mean that the money is in the bank or in the store. Included in this profit is the money due the owner from charge sales, and the larger the charge sales amount, the smaller the amount of cash in the till will be.

Also, from the net profit must come all ownership draws and equipment payments. If the owner were to draw out more than five thousand dollars during this period of business, it would not show on the Income Statement. It would, however, show on the Balance Sheet. When this happens, the amount of the owner's capital diminishes, and the net worth is reduced.

Many new owners do not understand that even if there is money in the bank, it might not belong to them. It could be money that should be used to pay creditors (suppliers), and if used, it could lead to serious problems.

With the knowledge you are acquiring through this book, I'm certain this calamity will not befall you.

Caution

Before we go any further into the theories of accounting, I want to delve into two other areas that can plague the bookkeeper. These are the Petty Cash Fund and reconciling the bank statement. Following are examples of both.

A Brief Pause

An unnecessary annoyance of the new office person is the need to reconcile a bank statement. It is a job which is really not that difficult. Balancing the bank statement is as easy as any other bookkeeping step. It is simply a matter of following a few specific steps, which will make the outcome a joy rather than a frustration.

Good accounting involves having a good routine. The employee who forms good habits will be rewarded with less work to accomplish a project than will the person who does a sloppy job. Many accountants like to make work for no other reason than to prove they are necessary to you. I was never able to look upon accounting that way because I'm lazy by nature and don't like extra work. I made my job as easy as possible, and did as little as I had to in order to do the job right. It is this attribute which brought about my flat-form ledger, and my method of doing things which makes it easier for the beginner.

The Bank Statement Arrives

Reconciling a bank statement is really a very simple matter. It needs to be done faithfully each month prior to organizing and tallying other accounting records.

Checking the Bank Statement

What to Do

To begin, arrange the cancelled checks in numerical order before attempting anything else. If there are a large number of checks, I suggest arranging them in piles in groups of ten (checks in the #410's, 420's, 430's, etc.). This way, you have very small piles to work with and it is easier than trying to hold two hundred checks in one hand while shuffling the numbers into the required position with the other.

Now, arrange each pile in numerical order, then put the piles together so you have one pile of checks. These are now in number sequence.

Refer to last month's Bank Reconciliation form which you have filed nearby. Tick off the checks that the bank has paid with this statement against the checks which appear as outstanding (not paid) from last month. Then tick off the remaining checks against the checks shown in this month's check distribution journal. Make certain the bank has paid the checks for the amounts they were written.

Start off this month with a new bank form and label it properly for future reference. (You can design your own form similar to Figure 22.) Insert the general ledger balance figure ($4,566.09) which is found in the column Total to Date under September. Insert the balance the bank shows as due you at the end of September ($4,149.72). Next, working from the cash and sales journal, trace every deposit into the bank statement. Again, make sure the dates and the amounts of the deposits agree with those appearing on the journal. In this instance, we see the deposits for September 29 and 30 were not processed by the bank until after September 30. List their values under the heading Add: Deposits in Transit. Total them and add to the bank balance. The reason for this is the money should have been in the bank at month's end if it were possible to have verified the money and actually deposited it before the close of bank business on September 30.

List on the reconciliation form all the checks written in previous months and in this month which the bank has not yet paid. List them under Checks Outstanding. You can see they total $443.87. Enter this amount in the upper right hand portion under the heading Less Checks Outstanding. Reason? If these checks had been presented to the bank not later than September 30, they would have been paid by the bank and accordingly deducted from the balance due the business. The result of the calculation must agree with the balance shown in the general ledger.

Except:

Service Charges

Are there bank service charges? Are there check charges for purchase of new checks? Any such charges are usually carried under a heading of "Bank Charges" in a small box at the bottom of the statement. If there are charges, these will have to be deducted from the statement before your bank balance and check register balance will agree. You will also need to make a journal entry on the charges to get them into the expenses of the business. This can be done by a journal entry or by writing them in on the bottom of the check register. Such charges *must also be deducted from the balance on your check book stub.*

If there is still a difference:

1. Check the amounts of returned checks against the figures in the check register. Are they the same?

2. Check the amounts of deposits shown on the statement with the deposit slips for those figures. Are they the same?

3. Check the additions and subtractions on your check stubs to be certain the deposits have been entered into your running balance properly. Was the remaining balance correct?

4. Check the amounts of returned checks against the figures shown as "Paid" on the statement. Are they the same?

5. Add up the amounts of the checks paid, plus charges, on the statement. Are the two figures the same?

6. Check your tape of outstanding checks again to be sure you have read the figures correctly. Are your new and old figures the same?

After going through all of this, if you can say "yes" to all of these items, your bank statement should reconcile.

Now that we have balanced the bank statement, place the checks and the statement back in the envelope, mark it for the month it covers in bright ink on the outside, and file it. File your reconciliation work sheet separately. This portion of your job is completed until next month, when you will go through it all over again. Just make sure to do it every month when the bank statement arrives, and you shouldn't have any problems. Be sure to enter bank charges into the proper account, either by placing on the check distribution or through a general journal entry.

Figure 22
Bank Reconciliation

Balance Per Bank Statement,		
September 30, 19____		$4,149.72
Add: Deposits in Transit		
September 29	$365.02	
September 30	495.22	
		$ 860.24
Less: Checks Outstanding		
No. 269	$ 27.25	
No. 273	52.25	
No. 278	116.09	
No. 283	142.22	
No. 291	106.06	
		$ 443.87
Balance Per General Ledger,		
September 30, 19____		$4,566.09
Balance, Reconciled, Per Bank,		
September 30, 19____		$4,566.09
Difference To Be Accounted For		$ -0-

So You Need Some Petty Cash

In many businesses, it is necessary to have funds on hand to make small purchases without the need for a check for each purchase. This is handled through the use of a Petty Cash Fund.

One occurrence which should be declared a disaster for any bookkeeper is to have the United Parcel truck stop by some afternoon to deliver a parcel with a Cash on Delivery charge. The immediate result is a deep feeling of panic and a quick scramble to find enough funds to pay the driver. You can probably still remember the panicky search through desk drawers in hopes of finding a few coins. Then comes the mad dash next door to see if Helen, the beauty parlor operator, has eighty-five cents you can borrow.

Another version of that scene is having the boy who works in the back room sweeping, washing windows and the like, come in to demand money to buy soap, brushes, a mop, and other utensils. Your pockets are already depleted from yesterday's onslaught, and you are ready to pull your hair out.

Even in the case of a store where there is an available supply of cash in the register, it is better to have a fund in the office to pay such needs than to delve into the till to take care of them. The Petty Cash Fund is the answer.

Some offices do not deal directly with the public and have no such source of cash on which to fall back. In such a case, it is good business practice to create a source which can be used to pay "petty bills." Having a working fund can save you from the annoyance of seeking cash in a hurry.

How to Set Up a Petty Cash Fund

Money for such a fund is obtained by writing a check on the general account and placing the cash in a box as a working amount. An amount of $25 to $200 can be acquired and is usually stored in a metal cash box with a lock and key. This box is usually placed in the office person's desk drawer and is accounted for by him or her.

Such cash is carried on the Balance Sheet in the assets section under the same heading of Cash on Hand as is the general checking account. The checking account is designated as Cash on Hand—Bank and the Petty Cash Fund as Cash on Hand—Petty Cash Fund. Naturally, the checking amount varies on the statement from month to month, but the petty cash fund amount does not unless it is increased or decreased according to need.

In doling out the cash for miscellaneous purchases (office supplies, restroom items, cleaning materials, minor tools, etc.), the party making the purchase can either buy the item and present a sales slip for reimbursement, or ask for money in advance to make the purchase and return the change with a sales receipt. Be sure to keep the slip and mark it as to its use. Place it in an envelope under the coin tray in the cash box.

Reconciling the Petty Cash Fund

Every so often the funds spent need to be replaced and the cash box needs to be reconciled. This is accomplished in the following manner:

First: Count the money remaining in the cash fund and mark down the total on a scratch pad. Subtract that total from the total amount of the fund. The difference is the amount of money that should be represented by the register tags and cash slips in your envelope.

Second: Segregate the slips and invoices by kind of expense (office supplies, cleaning supplies, gasoline, auto expense, freight-in, freight-out, merchandise delivered COD, maintenance costs, etc.). This should give you a number of small piles.

Third: Add up each pile individually, total, and attach the adding machine tape (or a piece of scratch paper) to the pile. Mark on the tape what item of expense the pile of slips is charged to (gasoline, cleaning supplies, etc.). After this is accomplished, add up the totals of the individual piles and total. This figure should be the same as the amount you are looking for. It works out like this: cash fund amount minus total of cash remaining in the cash box. If it doesn't balance, don't panic. It could be more than the amount needed to reimburse the box, or it could be less. In the case of the figure being more than the box calls for, it indicates that someone purchased an item and returned too much cash or that the item purchased was less than the purchase slip calls for. In either case, in making up the check to reimburse the cash box, make the check out for the amount needed to restore the Petty Cash Fund to its original amount. Record any overage or shortage in the appropriate account.

Fourth: We new have the amount necessary for writing the check to pay back our cash box and to enter the expense amounts into our records.

Write the check. Attach the last adding machine tape (total of all the pile totals) to the check stub in the check book, write the account name beside each expense item amount, and proceed to post the figures to the various distribution columns across the check register. When completed, the amount of the check will agree with the amounts you have posted and your line will be in balance. Now, your check register and your cash box are both in balance. Here is an example of an overage situation mentioned above:

Example:		
Original amount in cash fund		$40.00
Two-week cash count		15.86
Difference in amount		$24.14

(We are supposedly looking for $24.14 in cash slips)

As cash expenditures, we could have the following:

Gasoline	$ 5.00
Office Supplies	3.85
Cleaning Supplies	4.69
UPS—Freight-in	8.32
Light bulbs	2.98
Total purchase slips and invoices	$24.84
Amount due box to reimburse	$24.14
Overage	$ .70

With completion of reconciling the cash box and posting the reimbursement check, you can now return the cash slips to their envelope, mark it with the date covered (April someteenth through April umpteenth), write the total on the outside (in this case $24.84), write the check number (in this case #345) and file the envelope away for future reference. Now you are ready for the IRS any time they desire to come.

7

Posting to the General Ledger from the General Journal

In all systems of bookkeeping and accounting, items come up which have no supporting entry to place them in the books. Such items could be inventory taxes levied on the employer, cash purchases which might be made out of the owner's pocket, and depreciation. There could be many more examples. Because such items do not appear on the cash and sales journal or the check distribution, it is necessary to have some other "instruments of original entry" to place these values into the books.

Another Instrument of Original Entry

Every item that is written into the ledger must have an instrument of entry. If such items as the cash purchases, the depreciation, or payroll taxes should be questioned, the auditor will want to know how it was calculated. The general journal is used to support the entry of such items.

We have completed our first serious Balance Sheet, which contains most of the expenses involved in operating a small business, except depreciation. I have saved this item until now in order to illustrate the use of the journal entry.

So now you can ask, "What is the journal entry?"

The General Journal: What It Is

The general journal is part of the general ledger. It is a group of sheets which is placed in the front of the ledger and is used for explaining items not entered in any of the daily journals (cash register, etc.). The amounts of the items involved are written in the general journal and then posted to the accounts to which they belong. Our depreciation on Hazel's truck and store fixtures gives an opportunity to illustrate how such entries are made.

The journal entry sheet is a printed form and is made in sizes to fit the popular hardbound ledger covers. Your office supply store will be pleased to help you pick out what you need to set up a regular set of books.

Set up four columns and mark them "Description," "Posting Reference," "Debits," and "Credits." Write the item which you are depreciating and show how the amount of money is calculated. Here again every value is entered twice, once to the debit side and once to the credit side. This is true of all three of our journal entries. Below the entries, explain why the items are entered in the general journal.

In posting money in the journal columns, always remember that the debits are always in the left hand column and credits in the right hand column. Because of this, debit figures are written in first so that they are above the credit entries.

In posting our journal entries into the general ledger, Figures 24 and 25, I have prepared a new column to receive them so that the auditor can tell at a glance where the items come from.

In posting our first item, "Depreciation—Truck," the debit figure of $20.35 is posted to the depreciation expense account, as instructed in the posting reference column. The credit is posted to the reserve for depreciation account. When this is completed, tick off the amounts on the journal sheet with red pencil and go on to the next item, "Depreciation—Fixtures." This is handled in the same manner as the truck depreciation, as is office equipment.

Now that you have finished posting the depreciation to our flatform ledger, carry the totals across to a new total column and be ready for your next month. The finished posting should look like the illustration in Figures 24 and 25.

Employer's Payroll Taxes

One of the frequent items to be handled in the general journal is the employer's portion of payroll taxes. Because we are working on the cash basis, we won't bother with it until the check is made out to the Internal Revenue. Then we will post the figure from the check as written on the stub. A good bookkeeper will always break down the amounts of tax which are covered by one check.

For example, if the income tax withheld for a quarter (three months) is $675.42, and the F.I.C.A. is $123.75, the employer must put up the same amount as the employee's F.I.C.A (or, in this case, another $123.75, which is included in the check which accompanies the quarterly return). This last amount is an expense to the employer and is entered as such in the books. If the bookkeeper writes down these amounts on the stub: WH-$675.42, FICA-$123.75, Emp. FICA-$123.75, then the employer's portion, or the last $123.75, can be posted directly to the payroll tax expense account from the check register at the end of the month.

So You're Going to Have a Payroll

Congratulations! Setting up a payroll is a big step in operating a business. First of all, it means that the business has grown so much that you can no longer do all the work yourself. It is a pleasure to hire someone to take some of the load off your shoulders.

It could mean that you are tired of going home at midnight each

Figure 23

GENERAL JOURNAL   SEPTEMBER 19——

DESCRIPTION	POSTING REFERENCE		DEBITS			CREDITS	
			5	6		7	8
DEPRECIATION—TRUCK	DEPRECIATION EXPENSE		2035				
	RESERVE FOR DEPRECIATION					2035	
DEPRECIATION—FIXTURES	DEPRECIATION EXPENSE		2250				
	RESERVE FOR DEPRECIATION					2250	
DEPRECIATION—OFFICE EQUIPMENT	DEPRECIATION EXPENSE		180				
	RESERVE FOR DEPRECIATION					180	
TO RECORD THE DEPRECIATION ON THE TRUCK, FIXTURES, & OFFICE EQUIPMENT							

4912½ BUFF · 8912½ GREEN · 4212½ WHITE

Figure 24

HAZEL'S BOUTIQUE — GENERAL LEDGER — SEPTEMBER, 19___

PAID OUTS (CHECK DIST.)	TOTAL FOR MONTH	TOTAL TO DATE	JOURNAL ENTRIES	TOTAL				
	1	2	3	4	5	6	7	
INSURANCE	12750	25250		25250				
TRUCK EXP.	3765	11352		11352				
ACCOUNTING	—	1000		1000				
OFFICE EXPENSE	2188	3768		3768				
DEPRECIATION			2035 2250					
PAYROLL TAX EXP.			180	4465				
TAXES & LICENSE		1750		1750				
INTEREST EXP.								
(OVER)/SHORT		(706)		(706)				
DUES — CONTRIB.								
(DISCOUNTS)								
(OTHER INCOME)								
MISC. EXP.	5430	7210		7210				

49 12¼ BUFF   89 12¼ GREEN   42 12¼ WHITE

Figure 25

HAZEL'S BOUTIQUE — GENERAL LEDGER — SEPTEMBER, 19___

ASSETS			TOTAL FOR MONTH	TOTAL TO DATE	JOURNAL ENTRIES	NEW TOTAL		
CASH IN BANK				367862		367862		
ACCOUNTS RECEIVABLE								
RESERVE FOR BAD DEBTS								
INVENTORY								
PREPAID EXP.				8900		8900		
DEPOSITS				5000		5000		
EQUIPMENT-TRUCK				97683		97683		
RESERVE FOR DEPRECIATION					2035	2035		
FIXTURES & FURNITURE				180000		180000		
RESERVE FOR DEPRECIATION					2250	2250		
OFFICE EQUIPMENT				14960		14960		
RESERVE FOR DEPRECIATION					180	180		
LEASEHOLD IMPROVEMENTS								
AMORTIZATION								

4912½ BUFF · 8912½ GREEN · 4212½ WHITE

night and getting up at four-thirty the next morning in order to get the store cleaned before the day's business begins. It means that someone else will do the hard work. Now you can utilize your talents in getting bigger and bigger sales and still have a little time to spend an evening or two at home with your family.

Having a payroll also means other things.

It means getting employer numbers from the federal government (Internal Revenue Service) and from the state in which you do business (The Department of Benefit Payments in California) It also means withholding money from your employee's paychecks for income tax and social security, for the IRS and state disability insurance, and income tax for your state. You might also need to withhold additional money for whatever might be required for your state, county, and/or city. It means filling out forms for both state and federal governments so that you will have their sanction to make withholdings from the employee's checks. You will then be able to transmit the money to them at the end of the quarter.

Making Deposits

In most cases, if you withhold more than five hundred dollars in any one quarter, you must deposit it at a federal deposit bank. The IRS furnishes forms to be used in making these deposits. (If the withholding for one quarter does not come to five hundred dollars, then you do not have to deposit taxes. You may pay the taxes to IRS with form 941, or you may deposit them by the end of the next month.)

Forms for making payroll deposits are mailed to the business owner at the beginning of each quarter and are to be used over the course of the three months involved. Making the deposits is a simple procedure. The amounts needed for the deposit can be taken directly from the check-distribution sheet, as will be explained on the following pages.

So get your forms from the state and IRS, fill them out and send them in. The addresses of the various state tax agencies are in the next chapter. You can get the IRS forms by contacting your local IRS office or by calling 1-800-424-FORM. In the meantime, you can hire whomever you please, so long as the party has a social security number and you verify that the employee is not an unauthorized alien. You should get the "Handbook for Employers" from the Immigration and Naturalization Service by contacting your local INS office or calling 1-800-777-7700. Without the social security number, you have no way of turning in the tax money you withhold from wages. Such money does not belong to the store. It belongs to the employee and must be sent to the state and federal departments to which it is destined.

A number of new business ventures are closed because the owner fails to deposit or mail in withholding deposits. My word of caution to the business with a new payroll would be: "Do with the vendor's money as you will, but keep your nose clean with the Internal Revenue Service!"

To apply for an employer identification number you need Form SS-4 "Application for Employer Identification Number." The form is available from your local office of either the IRS or the Social Security Administration. You might also want to get a copy of IRS Publication 583, "Information for Business Taxpayers." In this book I have reproduced samples of the federal and state quarterly tax returns, and a quarterly sales tax form. As stated before, the forms vary from state to state, but this gives you some idea of what information is required and how to fill them in. The federal form should be the same as in the example.

So now you have applied for an employer's number and have interviewed applicants for the job you are creating. All that is left is signing the employee and telling him or her to report to work.

Be sure the person you hire has a social security number or has applied for one!

Be sure to have your employee sign a W-4 form (as illustrated), giving you the information needed to withhold the amount of income tax she or he will have to pay. This is based on individual circumstances. Then you will need a withholding guide from the Internal Revenue Service, which is called "Circular E Employer's Tax Guide." This can be obtained by visiting or calling any IRS office. Because many states have an income tax withholding program, you will need an Employer's Tax Guide from them. If in doubt as to what the requirements are for your state, contact the proper department of your state government, and they will be pleased to help you.

In preparing the manuscript for this book, I contacted the Internal Revenue Service and the State Department of Benefit Payments in California. Both departments were happy to give me blank copies of their tax forms and lists of records needed by the employer.

Caution

Many small "cottage-type" business owners are plagued by people who want jobs and plead that the owner need not withhold any income tax money from them. It sounds very tempting, because if the owner does not withhold taxes to be sent to the IRS, it means escaping the owner's donation (FICA) to that department on the total taxable wages paid to the employee. (The owner sends in the same amount of money for social security for the employee as is held from the employee's wages.) It is calculated on the tax form by taking double the percentage amount that is charged the employee. If the percentage is 7.51 as it is for 1988 and 1989 (7.65 percent for 1990), the tax return instructs the owner to enter twice the percentage (15.02%; 15.30% in 1990) of the total taxable wages. This is the amount sent to the IRS.

The state also requires that unemployment insurance be paid on taxable wages. This amount usually is around 3.9% to 4.9%, depending on the employer and how much of a turnover he has in employees. This amount is not deducted from employee wages, but is an additional expense to the employer. When the employee states that you don't have to withhold tax money and needn't pay the additional FICA and Unemployment Insurance, it sounds very tempting.

Don't do it!

People have a way of quitting when you least expect it. Your employee might work for many months then find it necessary to quit because of family matters or some such thing. Usually, the first thing they do is to go to the state employment office and sign up for benefits. Immediately, the state sends an investigator around to learn why the required withholding taxes and unemployment insurance hasn't been turned in on the employee. In some states, they will calculate the amount and make you pay it on the spot.

Insist that the employee fill out a W-4 withholding form and state how many deductions you should allow in calculating the withholding taxes. FICA and State Disability will always be calculated by a

Form **W-4** (Rev. January 1984)	Department of the Treasury — Internal Revenue Service **Employee's Withholding Allowance Certificate**	OMB No. 1545-0010

1 Type or print your full name
MARY LOUISE WILSON

2 Your social security number
541 - 42 - 7361

Home address (number and street or rural route)
1812 FRONT STREET

City or town, State, and ZIP code
SANTA CRUZ, CALIFORNIA 95060

3 Marital Status
☐ Single ☒ Married
☐ Married, but withhold at higher Single rate
Note: If married, but legally separated, or spouse is a nonresident alien, check the Single box.

4 Total number of allowances you are claiming (from line F of the worksheet on page 2) 2

5 Additional amount, if any, you want deducted from each pay . . . . . $

6 I claim exemption from withholding because (see instructions and check boxes below that apply):

a ☐ Last year I did not owe any Federal income tax and had a right to a full refund of **ALL** income tax withheld, **AND**

b ☐ This year I do not expect to owe any Federal income tax and expect to have a right to a full refund of **ALL** income tax withheld. If both a and b apply, enter the year effective and "EXEMPT" here ▶ Year

c If you entered "EXEMPT" on line 6b, are you a full-time student? . . . . . . ☐ Yes ☐ No

Under penalties of perjury, I certify that I am entitled to the number of withholding allowances claimed on this certificate, or if claiming exemption from withholding, that I am entitled to claim the exempt status.

Employee's signature ▶ Mary Louise Wilson   Date ▶   , 19

7 Employer's name and address (Employer: Complete 7, 8, and 9 only if sending to IRS)
HAZEL'S BOUTIQUE
921 HAYWOOD DR. SANTA CRUZ, CA 95062

8 Office code

9 Employer identification number
94-1669471

- - - - - - - - - Detach along this line. Give the top part of this form to employer, keep the lower part for your records -

Privacy Act and Paperwork Reduction Act Notice.—If you do not give your employer a certificate, you will be treated as a single person with no withholding allowances as required by law. We ask for this information to carry out the Internal Revenue laws of the United States. We may give the information to the Dept. of Justice for civil or criminal litigation and to the States and the District of Columbia for use in administering their tax laws.

Purpose.—The law requires that you complete Form W-4 so that your employer can withhold Federal income tax from your pay. Your Form W-4 remains in effect until you change it or, if you entered "EXEMPT" on line 6b above, until February 15 of next year. By correctly completing this form, you can fit the amount of tax withheld from your wages to your tax liability.

If you got a large refund last year, you may be having too much tax withheld. If so, you may want to increase the number of your allowances on line 4 by claiming any other allowances you are entitled to. The kinds of allowances, and how to figure them, are explained in detail below.

If you owed a large amount of tax last year, you may not be having enough tax withheld. If so, you can claim fewer allowances on line 4, or ask that an additional amount be withheld on line 5, or both.

If the number of withholding allowances you are entitled to claim decreases to less than you are now claiming, you must file a new W-4 with your employer within 10 days.

The instructions below explain how to fill in Form W-4. **Publication 505**, Tax Withholding and Estimated Tax, contains more information on withholding. You can get it from most IRS offices.

For more information about who qualifies as your dependent, what deductions you can take, and what tax credits you qualify for, see the Form 1040 Instructions.

You may be fined $500 if you file, with no reasonable basis, a W-4 that results in less tax being withheld than is properly allowable. In addition, criminal penalties apply for willfully supplying false or fraudulent information or failing to supply information requiring an increase in withholding.

Line-By-Line Instructions

Fill in the identifying information in Boxes 1 and 2. If you are married and want tax withheld at the regular rate for married persons, check "Married" in Box 3. If you are married and want tax withheld at the higher Single rate (because both you and your spouse work, for example), check "Married, but withhold at higher Single rate" in Box 3.

Line 4 of Form W-4

Total number of allowances.—Use the worksheet on page 2 to figure your allowances. Add the number of allowances for each category explained below. Enter the total on line 4.

If you are single and hold more than one job, you may not claim the same allowances with more than one employer at the same time. If you are married and both you and your spouse are employed, you may not both claim the same allowances with both of your employers at the same time. To have the highest amount of tax withheld, claim "0" allowances on line 4.

A. Personal allowances.—You can claim the following personal allowances:

1 for yourself, 1 if you are 65 or older, and 1 if you are blind.

If you are married and your spouse either does not work or is not claiming his or her allowances on a separate W-4, you may also claim the following allowances: 1 for your spouse, 1 if your spouse is 65 or older, and 1 if your spouse is blind.

B. Special withholding allowance.—Claim the special withholding allowance if you are single and have one job or you are married, have one job, and your spouse does not work. You may still claim this allowance so long as the total wages earned on other jobs by you or your spouse (or both) is 10% or less of the combined total wages. Use this special withholding allowance only to figure your withholding. Do not claim it when you file your return.

C. Allowances for dependents.—You may claim one allowance for each dependent you will be able to claim on your Federal income tax return.

Note: *If you are not claiming any deductions or credits, skip D and E, add lines A, B, and C, enter the total on line F and carry the total over to line 4 of W-4.*

Before you claim allowances under D and E, total your non-wage taxable income (interest, dividends, self-employment income, etc.) and subtract this amount from estimated deductions you would otherwise enter in D1. If your non-wage income is greater than the amount of estimated deductions, you cannot claim any allowances under D. Moreover, you should take one-third of the excess (non-wage income over estimated deductions) and add this to the appropriate "A" value in Table 1 of determining allowances under E.

D. Allowances for estimated deductions.—If you expect to itemize deductions, you can claim additional withholding allowances. See Schedule A (Form 1040) for deductions you can itemize.

You can also count deductible amounts you pay for (1) alimony (2) qualified retirement contributions including IRA and Keogh (H.R. 10) plans (3) moving expenses (4) employee business expenses (Part I of Form 2106) (5) the deduction for a married couple when both work (6) net losses shown on Schedules C, D, E, and F (Form 1040), the last line of Part II of Form 4797, and the net operating loss carryover (7) penalty on early withdrawal of savings and (8) charitable contributions for nonitemizers. **Note:** Check with your employer to see if any tax is being withheld on moving expenses or IRA contributions. Do not include these amounts if tax is not being withheld; otherwise, you may be underwithheld. For details, see **Publication 505**.

The deduction allowed a married couple when both work is 10% of the lesser of $30,000 or the qualified earned income of the spouse with the lower income.

Once you have determined these deductions, enter the total on line D1 of the worksheet on page 2 and figure the number of withholding allowances for them.

E. Allowances for tax credits.—If you expect to take credits like those shown on lines 41 through 48 on the 1983 Form 1040 (child care, residential energy, etc.), use the table on the top of page 2 to figure the number of additional allowances you can claim. You may estimate these credits. Include the earned income credit if you are not receiving advance payment of it, and any excess social security tax withheld. Also, if you expect to income average, include the amount of the reduction in tax because of averaging when using the table.

percentage of gross taxable wages. Unemployment insurance is paid solely by the employer.

Of course, I would be remiss if I did not mention the case of an independent contractor. This is a person who has his/her own business and works for you along with several other clients. This person pays his/her own taxes under a "self-employed" status, and you are not required to withhold taxes to make employer contributions. Salespeople who travel usually work under this arrangement. A typing service might also operate this way, as well as moonlighting bookkeepers and accountants. Sometimes free-lance writers and advertising people prefer this arrangement, as well.

Independent Contractors

If you have an independent contractor doing work for you, it is probably safest to have a written agreement stating the facts as they are. It can be a simple letter agreement from the independent contractor to you, stating that the person has his or her own business and will not be considered your employee. The contractor will be working for several other clients (they do not need to be mentioned in the letter), will provide his/her own working space and tools, and will not be paid a salary. The rate of remuneration will depend on the actual work produced. Sometimes the independent contractor will bill you by the hour, but I tend to believe that it's better to pay by the unit of work.

For example, let's say that you have contracted with a woman to do some typing that is piling up. She has her own typewriter and will come to your business and pick up the work, take it home and do it, then deliver it to you when it's finished. You could pay her by the hour, but it would be better to pay her by the page, or on a per-letter basis. If you pay her by the hour, the IRS might rule that she is a part-time employee and you are liable for her withholding taxes. It is always better to have the contractor do the work at his/her own home or place of business rather than coming into your office. This is a formality, but it makes the independent contractor arrangement more credible to the IRS.

There are many free-lance, independent contractors operating their own businesses quite successfully. There might come a time when they would be very useful to you. When you have work for someone to perform on an uneven basis (the typing piling up, for example), they are convenient and worthwhile. Here are a few guidelines to bear in mind when working with an independent contractor in order to avoid misunderstandings with the IRS:

The Written Agreement

1. Always have a written agreement.

2. Make sure that the independent contractor is aware that he/she is not a part of your business, but has a separate business of his/her own.

3. Pay on a piece-meal basis, rather than by the hour or week.

4. Question the independent contractor about other clients he might have, or might be seeking in addition to you.

5. Require that the work be performed in his own home or place of business, using his own tools or equipment.

Guidelines for Independent Contractors

Now, let's get back to the more probable situation of your new full- or part-time employee. This person will be working in your office or place of business, using tools and equipment which you provide, and whom you will be paying on an hourly or weekly basis, or on a salary arrangement.

Employee Compensation Records

Now that you have an employee, you will need to keep records of his/her wages. This is so that you will have the information necessary to fill out your quarterly reports to the state and federal governments. Office supply stores carry sheets which are called "Employee Compensation Records." The one I happen to have is a Wilmer Service Line Form #25-F, but similar sheets are carried by all supply stores. For the small business, I have always set up my records on my old standby columnar pad, which serves just as well and is much less expensive (Burrough H 556).

After working out a few paychecks, we will post them to our improvised compensation sheet. You can then see how it works in preparing the totals for the quarterly tax returns.

In starting our payroll, we have signed Mary Louise Wilson on a W-4 withholding form so that we know how many deductions to take in making up her checks. We have also a verified address and social security number as required by the Internal Revenue. We are now ready to pay our young lady for her first week of work.

Figuring Net Pay

In making up the first paycheck, let us assume that Mary Wilson is to receive $5.00 per hour and has worked thirty-five hours this first week. A simple calculation of 35 hours times $5.00 gives a gross total of $175.00. Mary has indicated that she wishes to take two deductions (for herself and one dependent), so we look in our Federal Circular E Employer's Tax Guide in the "weekly-married" section for wages. We find this on page 26. Now we look for the gross figure of $175.00, which appears in the column "At least $175, but less than $180." Move your finger along the line of figures to the right to the "2 allowances" column and find that the given tax is $7.00. This is Mary's income tax withholding on her wages for the week.

The next figure we need is her FICA or Social Security withholding. This can be obtained by multiplying her gross wages by 7.51%. Doing so gives an answer of $13.14. This is the amount of her FICA withholding for the week. This figure can also be found by looking in the back of the Schedule E tax guide under "Social Security Employee Tax Tables." The figure for her gross wages of $175.00 will be found on page 41 of this booklet. In the future, we will use these tax guides more because it is the easiest way to learn the proper use of the booklet.

The above figures are for our federal withholding. Now we need to do the same thing for the state tax return. In California, there is a State Disability Insurance that is paid by the employee at the rate of 1% of the the gross wages up to $9,000.00. The amount that Hazel must withhold from Mary's wages would be $1.75, or 1% of $175.00. We also have a state income tax withholding program which is handled in the same manner as the federal withholding. If you have such a program in your state, you will be able to obtain a withholding booklet tax guide for the employer from them. If you have a state tax, look in the tax guide in the weekly pay section under "married persons." Look down the column on the left to the amount of "At least $170, but less than $180," move your finger across the columns until you come to the "2 allowances" column. We find that the amount is blank. This means that no state tax will be withheld on the gross wage of $175.00 when the worker has two deductions. (Yet, there will be state tax due on wages paid to Mary of $190 and above.)

So now we can make up the paycheck.

Getting Checks Printed

In having checkbooks made up for a business, it is always a good thing to look ahead and obtain the type of checks which will give the most information. The banks will have checks printed with most any kind of stub. They also have forms showing a stub that remains on the check. These have space for marking in the amounts of withholding from the employee's earnings. The employee MUST be given a record of his/her deductions from the check. It can be in the shape of a stub attached to the check, or in a small printed slip which can be obtained from office-supply stores. Such slips must show the gross wages, all of the deductions, and the net amount of the check.

In making up the check, *be sure to write down on the checkbook stub* the gross wages, the amount of the WH (federal income-tax withholding), FICA (social security), SDI (state disability), and S-WH (state income-tax withholding). The checkbook stub is that portion which remains in the checkbook. These figures must be posted to the check register and could be in error if not posted properly on the checkbook stub.

Such a posting might look this way:

HAZEL'S BOUTIQUE

Date: _OCTOBER 17, 19—_

Balance _$765.73_

Check No. _476_

Made to: _MARY L. WILSON_   _35 HRS._

_WH — $7.00_   FICA _$13.14_

SDI — $1.75   SWH _$0_

GROSS WAGES OWED $175.00 LESS

DEDUCTIONS OF $21.89 $153.11

Check Amt. _$153.11_

Balance _$612.62_

Deposits _−0−_

The Check Stub

The amount of Mary's take-home pay is $153.11 ($175.00 minus $7.00 federal WH, minus $13.14 FICA, AND $1.75 SDI = $153.11). Now that we have calculated the withholding and have a record in the checkbook, we can write the check and enter this information on our compensation record.

I have made up a payroll compensation sheet for the three months of the fourth quarter. For the first month, we assumed that Mary worked thirty-five hours the first week, forty hours the second and third weeks, and thirty-eight hours the fourth week. In making up the withholding and posting it to our compensation record, we find that she had a total of $765.00 earned, $38.00 federal income tax withheld, $57.45 FICA, $7.65 SDI, $5.30 state income tax withheld, and a balance or total take-home pay of $656.60.

To carry the pretense a little further, I have filled out wages for the entire quarter; the full three months in October, November, and December. See Figure 26.

This is the information we need to prepare our tax returns for the fourth quarter. But how do these checks appear in the check register?

We will make up a new check-distribution sheet for the month of October and post the four checks given to Mary in that month. See Figure 27.

Posting the Payroll Check to the Check Distribution Sheet

Since we have covered the procedure of posting payment checks in the check register in previous examples, we can bypass the first three checks on our distribution sheet and dig right into the reasons for posting our payroll checks in the manner shown.

Why wouldn't it be a simple matter to post the total amount of the check in the bank column as well as in the wages column? Because the total wage of $175.00 isn't taken from the bank. The amount of the check which will be taken from the store's checking account is only $153.11.

Then why not post the $153.11 in the wages column and forget the withholding columns? Because this isn't the amount of the wages. Mary Louise Wilson earned $175.00 that week. That is the cost of using her to help sell the merchandise. The figure of $153.11 would give a false cost of goods sold and create more profit on which Hazel would have to pay taxes (her own income taxes).

If the employee's withholding is shown on his compensation sheet, isn't that enough? Not always. By posting the amount to the check distribution sheet, the liabilities of the company are put into the books at the same time the expense portion is entered. This is the worth of the double entry bookkeeping system.

By posting the amounts to the check record, the owner has a record of the money owed to the various government agencies. By keeping these records, he or she will know when the required amount is reached so that the proper deposits can be made. All of our posting work is to give you the information needed to supervise your business. Otherwise, there would be no need for the chore of keeping records.

All you would have to do would be to count the money from sales, thrust it into your favorite mattress, then go forth gaily to spend it for fun. The way it is, the IRS can walk into a store at any time and request to see the books. If you can display records that prove your sales, your expenses, the withholding taxes, etc., the IRS will give you a clean bill of

Figure 26

MARY LOUISE WILSON
1812 FRONT ST.
SANTA CRUZ, CA

HAZEL'S BOUTIQUE
SS # 541-42-7361
MARRIED - 2 DEPENDENTS

HOUR RATE $5.00
PHONE 423-1160

	Gross Wages	Fed. Income Tax	FICA	SDI	State Tax	Net Check
OCTOBER						
WEEK ENDING 7TH						
35 HRS. @ $5.00	17500	700	1319	175	-0-	15311
W.E. 14TH —						
40 HRS. @ $5.00	20000	1100	1502	200	180	17018
W.E. 21 ST. —						
40 HRS. @ $5.00	20000	1100	1502	200	180	17018
W.E. 29TH						
38 HRS. @ $5.00	19000	900	1427	190	170	16313
TOTAL FOR MONTH	76500	3800	5745	765	530	65660
NOVEMBER						
W.E. 5TH						
36 HRS @ $5.00	18000	700	1351	180	-0-	15769
W.E. 12TH						
40 HRS. @ $5.00	20000	1100	1502	200	180	17018
W.E. 19TH						
40 HRS. @ $5.00	20000	1100	1502	200	180	17018
W.E. 26 ST						
23 HRS. @ $5.00	11500	600	864	115	-0-	10521
TOTAL FOR MONTH	69500	2900	5219	695	360	60326
DECEMBER						
W.E. 7TH						
40 HRS. @ $5.00	20000	1100	1502	200	180	17018
W.E. 14TH						
40 HRS. @ $5.00	20000	1100	1502	200	180	17018
W.E. 21 ST						
36 HRS. @ $5.00	18000	700	1351	180	-0-	15769
W.E. 28TH						
16 HRS. @ $5.00	8000	-0-	601	80	-0-	7319
TOTAL FOR MONTH	66000	2900	4956	660	360	57124
TOTAL FOR QUARTER	212000	9600	15920	2120	1250	183110

Figure 27

HAZEL'S BOUTIQUE   CHECK DISTRIBUTION   OCTOBER 19___

	DATE	VENDOR	CHECK #	CREDIT BANK	FED. WH	FICA	STATE SDI	STATE WH	DISCOUNT EARNED	MDS. PURCHASED	FREIGHT IN	WAGES	ADV. EXP.	TRUCK & AUTO EXP.	UTILITIES EXP.	OFF. EXP.	FREIGHT OUT	MISC.	MISC.
1	10-3	WESTERN DISTRIB	4173	18390						18390									
2	10-5	STANDARD OIL	4174	3260										3260					
3	10-5	PACIFIC TELE.	4175	2750														2750	
4	10-7	MARY WILSON	4176	5311	700	1314	175	-0-				17500							
5	10-7	S&S TRADING	4177	2460							2460								
6	10-10	LEATHER GOODS, INC.	4178	26570					542	27132									
7	10-11	STRONG SHOE CO.	4179	9500						9500									
8	10-11	COUNTY DUMP	4180	600														600	
9	10-12	SANTA CRUZ SENT	4181	7680									7680						
10	10-14	MARY WILSON	4182	17008	1100	1502	200	180				20000							
11	10-17	BLAIR MFG. CO.	4183	26130					533	26623									
12	10-18	SEVERSON SIGNS	4184	3500									3500						
13	10-18	BICKER'S REPAIR	4185	1846										1846					
14	10-19	SAN LORENTO WATER	4186	2630											2630				
15	10-19	PACIFIC GAS & ELEC.	4187	1475											1475				
16	10-21	MARY WILSON	4188	17008	1100	1502	200	180				20000							
17	10-21	HAROLD STRONG	4189	1500														1500 CLEAN UP	
18	10-24	UNITED PARCEL	4190	368													368		
19	10-24	STATIONERY	4191	1179												1179			
20	10-24	POSTMASTER	4192	650												650			
21	10-26	MATTEL TAGS	4193	2650						2650									
22	10-26	UNITED PARCEL	4194	365							365								
23	10-28	MARY WILSON	4195	16812	920	1472	190	170				19000							
24	10-28	HAZEL HAYWORTH	4196	10000														10000 DRAW	
25	10-29	TOM DIXLEY - FIXCAR	4197	1850										1850					
26	10-29	ARNOLD STRONG	4198	41500														41500 RENT	
27																			
28				248552	5800	5745	765	530	1075	94335	2825	76500	11180	6875	4105	1829	368	62350	
29																			
30																			

health. The same might be true of the state agencies with which you have to deal.

At the end of the quarter, you need only to look at the total figures on your check register in order to determine whether you must make a deposit. If you have under $500 of wage withholding per quarter, you do not have to make a deposit; you may pay the accumulated liability when you file Form 941. Larger employers who hire several employees and have withholding liabilities of more than $500 per month have to make payroll tax deposits each month. The deposits are to be made at any commercial bank and should be made with Form 8109. Larger employers must make deposits even more frequently. Your state might have different rules for making income tax withholding deposits. Not to make these deposits is simply setting the stage for possible financial trouble later on. If the money is left in your checking account, you will use it for other things. When the time comes to remit it to the IRS or the state, you will find you don't have the money to do so. If this happens too many times, the IRS could put a lock on your door and you are out of business. It is a good thing to post all the information which is needed to help you know where you stand.

The second, third and fourth payroll checks are all posted to the check register in the same manner, using the information entered on the check stub. All of the federal withholding is placed on the federal column, the FICA in the FICA column, and the SDI in the SDI column. If there had been state income tax involved, we would have posted that to the state tax column.

In examining the totals at the bottom of the page, you will find that the totals of the tax-withholding columns equal the totals of the first month (October) on the employee-compensation sheet. It is always a good practice to check the totals of one against the other. Even if there are a number of employees, it is a simple matter to recap them on a work sheet and compare the totals. Sometimes a mistake has been made and this is the first inkling that there is an error in your work.

Quarterly Reporting

At the end of the quarter (and at the end of the year), the compensation sheets should be recapped so that a total of all the employees is obtained. The totals for the year should equal the totals of all four quarter returns. The totals for the quarter should equal the total of the columns of the three month's check-register sheets when added together.

If this is done, when the W-2 forms are made up from the individual employee-compensation sheets, the total of all of them will equal the totals of the twelve check-distribution sheets for the year. They will also equal the totals of the four quarterly returns for the same period.

All of this double-checking pays off with accurate information in preparing the quarterly returns. If it is the last quarter of the year, then we prepare the W-2 forms. The transmittal form which MUST ACCOMPANY the W-2's when mailed to the state and federal agencies is also filled in. You will be penalized if you forget to mail the transmittal form.

If you have waded through all of this and are still with me, this is a good time to leap feet first into the governmental tax maze and see if we can fill out the form with the information we have on our employee

---

*For even larger companies, the deposits may be made even more frequently.

record. We will assume that Mary only worked the three months shown on the sheet and was Hazel's only employee. If there had been more employees, the procedure would be the same. Only the amounts would be larger.

Since the federal tax return form should be the same all over the country, let's tackle it first and fill in the spaces with the information we have on our employee compensation sheet. All of the operations on the form are numbered and should make explanation of each step a lot easier. We will start with item 1.

1. Number of employees (exept household) employed in pay period that includes March 12th (first quarter only). Answer: no answer is needed, since this is for the first quarter only and our example is for the fourth quarter.

2. Total wages and tips subject to withholding, plus other compensation. Answer: $2,120.00 (Gross wage figure from our compensation sheet.)

3. Total income tax withheld from wages, tips, annuities, gambling, etc. Answer: $96.00 (Total Federal Withholding from our compensation sheet.)

4. Adjustment of withheld income tax for preceding quarters of calendar year. Answer: None (If you discover, after mailing the third quarter, that you had quoted too much or too little tax withheld from the employee's wages, this is the place to post the difference. If you reported too little, enter the difference and add it to the income tax withheld. If you reported too much, enter the overage here and deduct it from the income tax figure. The totals of the two figures should bring your total withholding figure back into balance.)

5. Adjusted total of income tax withheld. Answer: $96.00. (Since we have no adjustment, the total is the same as in 3.)

6. Taxable FICA wages paid.* Answer $2,120.00 x 15.02% tax = $318.42. (The rate is 7.51%. Double is 15.02%. The employee portion was .0751% of $2,120.00 or $159.20 Double that amount is $318.42.) **This is the amount the employer must remit to the IRS. Since the amount withheld from the employee was $159.20, this means the owner is paying $159.20 out of store funds.** (Remember? I told you this is the way it works!)

*The maximum FICA taxable wages are $45,000.00 for 1986, for a maximum annual FICA withholding of $3,379.50. The maximum FICA wages are indexed for inflation, so the maximum amount generally will rise each year. It is doubtful that the small shop owner would ever have an employee who would earn the maximum wage base amount in one year. Wages in this amount would usually be found only in the crafts or the professions.

7. Taxable tips reported. Answer: None (If the business is a bar, restaurant, night club or an operation where the employee receives tips from customers, those tips would be reported to the employer. You, as the employer, should take withholding out of them. It is required.)

8. Total FICA taxes. Answer: $318.42

9. Adjustments. Answer: None

10. Adjusted total of FICA taxes. Answer: $318.42

Form **941**	**Employer's Quarterly Federal Tax Return**	

(Rev. January 1984)
Department of the Treasury
Internal Revenue Service

OMB No. 1545-0029

Your name, address, employer identification number, and calendar quarter of return. (If not correct, please change.)

Name (as distinguished from trade name)   Date quarter ended

Trade name, if any   Employer identification number

Address and ZIP code

| T |
| FF |
| FD |
| FP |
| I |
| T |

If address is different from prior return, check here ▶

Record of Federal Tax Liability
(Complete if line 13 is $500 or more)

See the instructions under rule 4 on page 4 for details before checking these boxes.

Check only if you made eighth-monthly deposits using the 95% rule. ▶ ☐

Check only if you are a first-time 3-banking-day depositor. ▶ ☐

If you are not liable for returns in the future, write "FINAL" ▶
Date final wages paid ▶

Complete for First Quarter Only

1 a Number of employees (except household) employed in the pay period that includes March 12th ▶

b If you are a subsidiary corporation AND your parent corporation files a consolidated Form 1120, enter parent corporation's employer identification number (EIN) ▶

Date wages paid		Tax liability
Day		
1st-3rd	A	
4th-7th	B	
8th-11th	C	
12th-15th	D	
16th-19th	E	
20th-22nd	F	
23rd-25th	G	
26th-last	H	
I Total ▶		
1st-3rd	I	
4th-7th	J	
8th-11th	K	
12th-15th	L	
16th-19th	M	
20th-22nd	N	
23rd-25th	O	
26th-last	P	
II Total ▶		
1st-3rd	Q	
4th-7th	R	
8th-11th	S	
12th-15th	T	
16th-19th	U	
20th-22nd	V	
23rd-25th	W	
26th-last	X	
III Total ▶		
IV Total for quarter (add lines I, II, and III)		

(First month of quarter: A–H; Second month of quarter: I–P; Third month of quarter: Q–X)

2 Total wages and tips subject to withholding, plus other compensation ▶

3 a Income tax withheld from wages, tips, pensions, annuities, sick pay, gambling, etc. ▶

b Backup withholding ▶

c Total income tax withheld (add lines 3a and 3b) ▶

4 Adjustment of withheld income tax for preceding quarters of calendar year:

a From wages, tips, pensions, annuities, sick pay, gambling, etc. ▶

b From backup withholding ▶

c Total adjustments (add lines 4a and 4b) ▶

5 Adjusted total of income tax withheld (line 3c as adjusted by line 4c)

6 Taxable social security wages paid:
$ _____ X 13.7% (.137)

7 a Taxable tips reported:
$ _____ X 6.7% (.067)

b Tips deemed to be wages (see instructions):
$ _____ X 7% (.07)

8 Total social security taxes (add lines 6, 7a, and 7b)

9 Adjustment of social security taxes (see instructions) ▶

10 Adjusted total of social security taxes

11 Total taxes (add lines 5 and 10) ▶

12 Advance earned income credit (EIC) payments, if any ▶

13 Net taxes (subtract line 12 from line 11). This must equal line IV (plus line IV of Schedule A (Form 941) if you have treated backup withholding as a separate liability.)

14 Total deposits for quarter, including any overpayment applied from a prior quarter, from your records ▶

15 Undeposited taxes due (subtract line 14 from line 13). Enter here and pay to Internal Revenue Service ▶

16 If line 14 is more than line 13, enter overpayment here ▶ $ _____ and check if to be: ☐ Applied to next return, or ☐ Refunded.

Under penalties of perjury, I declare that I have examined this return, including accompanying schedules and statements, and to the best of my knowledge and belief it is true, correct, and complete.

Signature ▶   Title ▶   Date ▶

Please file this form with your Internal Revenue Service Center (see instructions on "Where to File").

Form **941** (Rev. 1-84)

Paperwork Reduction Act Notice.—We ask for this information to carry out the Internal Revenue laws of the United States. We need it to ensure that taxpayers are complying with these laws and to allow us to figure and collect the right amount of tax. You are required to give us this information.

Backup Withholding.— Beginning January 1, 1984, payers must generally withhold 20% of taxable interest, dividend, and certain other payments if payees fail to furnish payers with the correct taxpayer identification number. There are other circumstances where the payer is also required to withhold. This withholding is referred to as backup withholding. Please see **Form W-9,** Payer's Request for Taxpayer Identification Number, and the 1984 **Instructions for Form 1096** for more details.

Report backup withholding amounts on line 3b, Backup withholding, on the same Form 941 you use for reporting social security and income tax withholding. For tax deposit purposes, see the Specific Instructions in the right column.

Sick Pay.—Employers should include third-party payments in the tax return during which they received notification from the third-party payer. This includes both the line 6 entry and the entry in the Record of Federal Tax Liability. For example, if the third-party payer makes a payment to an employee at the end of March and properly notifies the employer of the payment in April, the employer should report the payment on the second quarter Form 941. The tax liability should be shown in the Record of Federal Tax Liability for the deposit period in which the notification was received.

Forms W-4.—Send in each quarter with Form 941 copies of any Forms W-4 received during this quarter from employees (1) claiming more than 14 withholding allowances or (2) claiming exemption from income tax withholding if their wages are expected to usually exceed $200 a week. Include on each copy your name, address, and employer identification number. Do not send copies for employees who no longer work for you.

If you want to use magnetic media to transmit W-4 data to the IRS, see Revenue Procedure 80-8 in Cumulative Bulletin 1980-1, page 592.

Base withholding on the Forms W-4 that you sent in unless IRS notifies you in writing to do otherwise.

Circular E explains the rules for withholding, paying, depositing, and reporting Federal income tax, social security taxes, and Federal unemployment (FUTA) tax. Circular A, Agricultural Employer's Tax Guide, explains different rules for employers who have farmworkers. Get these circulars free from IRS offices.

General Instructions

Purpose of Form.—To report:

● Income tax you withheld from wages, tips, annuities, supplemental unemployment compensation benefits, certain gambling winnings, and third-party payments of sick pay.

● Income tax withheld as backup withholding.

● Social security taxes.

Who Must File.—Employers who withhold income tax, social security taxes, or both must file Form 941 quarterly. Exceptions are:

● Employers who report only withheld income tax. These include State and local governments, payers of supplemental unemployment compensation benefits, and certain payers of pensions, annuities, and sick pay. These employers should use **Form 941E,** Quarterly Return of Withheld Federal Income Tax.

● Employers who report taxes on household employees' wages. Report on **Form 942,** Employer's Quarterly Tax Return for Household Employees. But if you are a sole proprietor and file Form 941 for business employees, you can include your household employees on it.

● Employers who report taxes on agricultural employees' wages. Report these on **Form 943,** Employer's Annual Tax Return for Agricultural Employees. Also use Form 943 to report taxes on wages of household employees in a private home on a farm operated for profit.

When to File.—File starting with the first quarter in which you are required to withhold income tax, or pay wages subject to social security taxes.

Quarter	Ending	Due Date
Jan.-Feb.-Mar.	March 31	April 30
Apr.-May-June	June 30	July 31
July-Aug.-Sept.	Sept. 30	Oct. 31
Oct.-Nov.-Dec.	Dec. 31	Jan.31

If you deposited all taxes when due for a quarter, you have 10 more days after the above due date to file.

After you file your first return, we will send you a form every 3 months. Please use this form. If you don't have a form, get one from an IRS office in time to file the return when due.

If you temporarily stop paying wages or your work is seasonal, file a return for each quarter. Do this even though you have no taxes to report. But if you go out of business or stop paying wages, file a final return. Be sure to fill in the lines above line 1.

If you sell or transfer your business, both you and the new owner must file a return for the quarter in which the change took place. Neither should report wages paid by the other. (An example of a transfer is when a sole proprietor forms a partnership or corporation.) If a change occurs, please attach to your return a statement that shows: New owner's name (or new name of the business); Whether the business is now a sole proprietorship, partnership, or corporation; Kind of change that took place (sale, transfer, etc.); Date of the change.

When a business is merged or consolidated with another, the continuing firm must file the return for the quarter in which the change took place. The return should show all wages paid for that quarter.

Where to File.—

If your legal residence, principal place of business, office, or agency is in	File with the Internal Revenue Service Center at
New Jersey, New York City and counties of Nassau, Rockland, Suffolk, and Westchester	Holtsville, NY 00501
New York (all other counties), Connecticut, Maine, Massachusetts, New Hampshire, Rhode Island, Vermont	Andover, MA 05501
Delaware, District of Columbia, Maryland, Pennsylvania	Philadelphia, PA 19255
Alabama, Florida, Georgia, Mississippi, South Carolina	Atlanta, GA 31101
Michigan, Ohio	Cincinnati, OH 45999
Arkansas, Kansas, Louisiana, New Mexico, Oklahoma, Texas	Austin, TX 73301
Alaska, Arizona, Colorado, Idaho, Minnesota, Montana, Nebraska, Nevada, North Dakota, Oregon, South Dakota, Utah, Washington, Wyoming	Ogden, UT 84201
Illinois, Iowa, Missouri, Wisconsin	Kansas City, MO 64999
California, Hawaii	Fresno, CA 93888
Indiana, Kentucky, North Carolina, Tennessee, Virginia, West Virginia	Memphis, TN 37501
If you have no legal residence or principal place of business in any State	Philadelphia, PA 19255

Employer Identification Number (EIN).—If you have not asked for a number, apply for one on **Form SS-4,** Application for Employer Identification Number. Get this form from IRS or Social Security Administration (SSA) offices.

If you do not have a number by the time a return is due, write "Applied for" and the date you applied in the space shown for the number. For more information concerning an EIN, see Publication 583, Information for Business Taxpayers.

Filing on Magnetic Media.—For information for tape filing of Form 941, see the revenue procedure titled Magnetic Tape Reporting; Form 941. You can get a copy by contacting an IRS office.

Penalties and Interest.—There are penalties for filing a return late and paying or depositing taxes late, unless there is reasonable cause. If you are late, please attach an explanation to your return. There is a penalty of 25% of the overstatement if, without reasonable cause, you overstate the amount you deposited. There are also penalties for willful failure to file returns and pay taxes when due, furnish statements to employees, keep records, and for filing false returns or submitting bad checks.

Interest is charged on taxes paid late at the rate set by law.

Specific Instructions

For tax deposit purposes, you can either combine backup withholding with other taxes reported on Form 941 and deposit the combined total, or you can treat backup withholding as a separate tax and deposit it separately following the same deposit rules used for social security and withheld income taxes.

If you treat backup withholding as a separate tax, show the amounts for deposit purposes on new **Schedule A (Form 941),** Record of Federal Backup Withholding Tax Liability, and when depositing these taxes, mark the "945" entry on the deposit coupon (see Depositing Taxes below). Schedule A (Form 941) must be attached to Form 941.

Completing the Record of Federal Tax Liability.—If your taxes for the quarter (line 13) are less than $500, you do not have to complete the Record. You may pay the taxes with Form 941 or deposit them by the due date of the return. If your taxes for the quarter are $500 or more, you **must** complete the Record.

Each month is divided into eight deposit periods that end on the 3rd, 7th, 11th, 15th, 19th, 22nd, 25th, and last day of the month as shown in the Record. If your taxes for every month are less than $3,000, you can show them on the Total lines (I, II, and III) and skip the other lines. If your taxes for any month are $3,000 or more, find the eighth-monthly period(s) during the quarter in which you had a payday. Make entries only on the lines next to these periods. (For example, if you pay wages on the 1st and 15th of each month, complete lines A, D, I, L, Q, T, and the monthly Total lines.)

Enter your tax liability (income tax withheld plus both the employee and employer social security taxes minus any Advance Earned Income Credit payments) for each eighth-monthly period during which you had a payday.

The total of the tax liability column, line IV (plus line IV on Schedule A (Form 941) if you treat backup withholding as a separate liability) must equal "Net taxes" (line 13). Otherwise you may be charged a penalty, based on your average tax liability, for not making deposits of taxes.

Taxpayers who willfully claim credit on line 14 for deposits not made are subject to fines and other criminal penalties.

How to Make Deposits.—In general, you must deposit backup withholding, income tax withheld, and both the employer and employee social security taxes with an authorized financial institution or a Federal Reserve bank or branch that serves your area. Use new **Form 8109,** Federal Tax Deposit Coupon, which must be included with each deposit, to indicate the type of tax being deposited. To avoid a possible penalty, do not mail your deposit directly to IRS. Records of your deposits will be sent to IRS for crediting to your business accounts.

There will no longer be periodic mailouts of Federal tax deposit forms. If you need additional coupons, use the FTD Reorder Form (**Form 8109A**) included in the coupon book. If you do not have a coupon book, please request one from your IRS district office. There are 15 coupons and a reorder form in each book and the coupons can be used to deposit any type of tax for any tax year. Please see the instructions in the front of the coupon book for additional information.

8

The State Quarterly Tax and Federal Tax Forms *

The kinds of taxes withheld and remitted to your state agencies may differ from the taxes we have in California. I'm certain, however, that the ones you do have require the same procedure in making out the forms. If you learn the procedure, a change in methods of making up your own state tax returns can be taken in stride. Complete instructions are normally included with a tax return form. If you understand the filling out of one, it should aid you in filling out the other.

Unemployment insurance is collected from the employer in all of our fifty states. Other taxes, such as state disability insurance and income tax, may be collected in your state. Everything is based on the information we have recorded on the employee's compensation sheet. Check the following items with the example state tax return.

Item A. Number of employees earning wages during the period which included the 12th day of the month.
Answer: First month, one; Second month, one; Third month, one. (If the owner had three people on the payroll, but only two were working on the 12th day of the given month, it would be marked "two".)

Item B. Total wages in subject employment.
Answer: $2,120.00 (This is a rehash of the federal question.)

Item C. Unemployment Insurance Taxable Wages.
Answer: $2,120.00 (Some employees earning higher wages will go beyond the maximum taxable wages. The amount of non-taxable wages must be recorded. This is an employer-paid tax, and you certainly don't want to pay more than the law requires. Mary Louise Wilson's wages were all taxable. Check with your state agency for the maximum taxable figure.)

Item D. Disability Insurance Taxable Wages.
Answer: $2,120.00 (The amount of wages that are taxable for un-employment in the state of California is $9,000.00. The employee pays 1% of gross wages up to this amount. Any wages over that amount should be recorded so that it can be deducted from the total wages paid for the quarter in question. Income tax is the only tax that is remitted to the government agencies in the exact amount taken from the employee's

*Please check with your local IRS office to verify the elements in this section, as recent changes in the Federal Tax Law may have affected their use in your situation.

check. All of the others are calculated *on the quarterly tax form and may vary from the actual amounts withheld.)*

Item E. Employer Contributions.
Answer: $82.68 (This is the nitty gritty. This is where the employer's donation is calculated, the amount paid into the state unemployment fund, and the employees are protected by the unemployment insurance provisions. The rate varies according to the employer and the employee turnover rates. In Hazel's case, the rate is 3.9% of taxable wages up to $7,000.00. The contribution is 3.9 times $2,120.00)

Item F. Employee Contributions.
Answer: $21.20 (One percent of $2,120.00)

Item G. Personal Income Tax Withheld
Answer: $12.50

Item H. Adjustments
Answer: None (This works in the same manner as the federal adjustments. In our present example, there are none.)

Item J. (There is no Item I.) Pay this amount.
Answer: $116.38 (This is an easy one. Add up what you owe: Items E, F, and G. Place the total in this space, make out a check, be sure to sign both check and quarterly return, and mail them.)

Item K. List of employees on your payroll.
Answer: Mary Louise Wilson, 541-42-7361, $2,120.00 (Enter the social security number, making sure it is correct, fill in the name and the gross amount of money the taxes are paid on.)

This completes the form. Since we have finished the fourth quarter returns, we might as well follow through by preparing the W-2 forms for the employee.

Caution

If, for some reason, the employer is not able to remit the amount of the withholding taxes at the time it is supposed to be mailed, send the form without the money. The law states that the form must be filed by the set date. If the employer mails the form without the money, he/she wil escape being penalized for not doing so, but will be charged interest for the length of time tardy in sending it.

To refrain from mailing the form is breaking the law. To mail it without the money is simply defaulting on the payment of the taxes.

The IRS will even give the storekeeper a time plan for making delinquent payments. Refusing to mail the form could cause the door to be padlocked.

I am certain that every person living in the United States who has worked for wages at any time is aware of the W-2 form. If a person obtains a job and works for only half a day, it is necessary for the employer to put him/her on a payroll and to withhold taxes from the earnings. If there is not any income tax, there will be FICA tax which must be withheld.

DE 3 CONTRIBUTION RETURN and REPORT OF WAGES Under the UNEMPLOYMENT INSURANCE
CODE and REPORT OF CALIFORNIA PERSONAL INCOME TAX WITHHELD

STATE OF CALIFORNIA, DEPARTMENT OF BENEFIT PAYMENTS, 800 CAPITOL MALL, SACRAMENTO, CA 95814

Corrections in name or address should be made in the address reading below.
Ownership Changes should be reported on the reverse side.

				YR	QTR
QUARTER ENDED DEC. 31, 19___	DUE JAN. 15, 19___	DELINQUENT IF NOT MAILED BY JAN. 31, 19___		19__	4

HAZEL HAYWORTH   190 8847
DBA/ HAZEL'S BOUTIQUE   3.9
921 HAYWOOD DRIVE
SANTA CRUZ, CA 95062

190 8957

	BAT	EFFECTIVE DATE	WIC	

YOU MUST FILE THIS RETURN EVEN THOUGH YOU HAD NO PAYROLL THIS QUARTER. IF YOU HAD NO PAYROLL SHOW "NONE" IN ITEM B AND SIGN THE CERTIFICATE.

A. No. of employees earning wages during pay periods which include the 12th day of: R
1ST MO. OF QTR. ___ 1   2ND MO. OF QTR. ___ 1   3RD MO. OF QTR. ___ 1

B. TOTAL WAGES IN SUBJECT EMPLOYMENT . . . . (B)	2,120	00
C. UNEMPLOYMENT INSURANCE TAXABLE WAGES (Individual Employee Wages To $ See Instructions). (C)	2,120	00
D. DISABILITY INSURANCE TAXABLE WAGES (Individual Employee Wages To $ See Instructions). (D)	2,120	00
E. EMPLOYER CONTRIBUTIONS (3.9 % times C). . . . . (E)	82	68
F. EMPLOYEE CONTRIBUTIONS (Ee Contr) (1.0% x D) $ ___ − ___ = Enter Difference (F) LESS Ee Contr Previously Paid This Qtr.	21	20
G. CALIF. PERSONAL INCOME TAX WITHHELD (PIT)(G1) $ ___ − ___ = Enter Difference (G2) LESS PIT Previously Paid This Qtr.	12	50
H. ADJUSTMENTS: Increase		
Decrease.		
J. PAY THIS AMOUNT (Items E, F, G2 and H) ─────────────────▶ (J)	116	38

MAKE CHECK PAYABLE TO DEPT. OF BENEFIT PAYMENTS   Bank No. ___

BE SURE TO SIGN THIS CERTIFICATE   *I CERTIFY that the information herein is true and correct to the best of my knowledge and belief.*
DATE JAN. 15, 19___ SIGNATURE *Hazel Hayworth* TITLE (OWNER, ETC.) OWNER

List your employees below IF THERE IS ENOUGH SPACE FOR ALL OF THEM. You may single space to list as many as 18 below. If this is not enough space, LIST NONE BELOW — Use Continuation Sheets DE 3B for your ENTIRE LIST. Continuation sheets may be obtained from any Employment Tax District Office.

Social Security Account Number 000 00 0000	Employee Name First Name	Middle Initial	Last Name	M. Total Wages Paid This Qtr. Dollars	Cents
541 42 7361	MARY	L.	WILSON	2,120.00	
N. Total of this page OR total of continuation sheets attached. (See Instructions)				2,120.00	

*Please check with your state's IRS office for the proper form and
procedure, as these examples are based on California's tax law.

DE 43A	CALIFORNIA	RECONCILIATION OF INCOME TAX WITHHELD AND TRANSMITTAL OF FORMS W-2	

1. Total California income tax withheld as reported on Forms W-2/W-2P ⟶ **$ 12.50** | 3 NUMBER OF FORMS W-2/W-2P (COPY 1) WAGE AND TAX STATEMENTS, ATTACHED

2. Total California income tax withheld as reported on Quarterly Contribution Returns:
   a. March 31 . . . $ **-0-**   b. June 30 . . . $ **-0-**
   c. Sept. 30 . . . **-0-**   d. Dec. 31 . . . **12.50**
   If Line 1 and Line 2 totals are different, see instruction 3 on reverse side.

TOTAL LINES 2A THRU 2D **12.50** $

NUMBER OF FORMS: **1**

Under penalties of perjury, I declare that this return and attached statements are true, correct, and complete.

Date **JAN. 15, 19—** Signature *Hazel Hayworth* Title **OWNER**

Type or Print Employer's Name and Address as it appears on Quarterly Contribution Return

Name **HAZEL HAYWORTH DBA/HAZEL'S BOUTIQUE**
Street Address **921 HAYWOOD DR.**
City, State, and ZIP Code **SANTA CRUZ, CA 95062**

DBP Account No. (from Quarterly Contribution Return)

Department of Benefit Payments
P.O. Box 105
Sacramento, California 95801

DE 43A (9-74)   DUP ① △ OBP

Attach tape and mail this copy, with Forms W-2/W-2P per instruction 9
ADDRESS MUST SHOW THROUGH WINDOW OF ENVELOPE

INSTRUCTIONS (REVERSE SIDE DE 43 AND DE 43A)

1. **WHO MUST FILE** — Each employer who has paid wages in California during the year (attach to W-2/W-2P forms).

2. **PURPOSE** — To reconcile withheld California Income Tax reported on quarterly returns with amounts reflected on attached W-2/W-2P forms, copy 1.

3. **RECONCILIATION** — (Includes corrections or adjustments to be made).
   a. Attach a machine tape (adding or Data Processing) showing the total California Income Tax withheld as reflected on enclosed W-2's/W-2P's and enter this total on Line 1. Line 2 should agree with amounts withheld as shown on each quarterly return (lines 2a through 2d). If totals on Lines 1 and 2 are different, attach a complete explanation.
   b. Submit only one DE 43/DE 43A for each employer account number. (If corrections are to be made, see Items c. and d. below.)
   c. If you have withholding adjustments to be made, please add/subtract (as the case may be) the amount previously over/under-reported in the current year from your withholding liability for the 4th quarter report, or attach a complete explanation. (Do not make your adjustment on your reports for the following year.)
   d. If you report an erroneous Social Security number, submit a corrected W-2/W-2P only. If you have an address or account number

correction for the DE 43/DE 43A, please make the correction on the original 43/DE 43A or attach the information. (Do not submit another DE 43/DE 43A.)

4. **WHEN TO FILE** — By the last day of February for the preceding calendar year or within 10 days of discontinuing business.

5. **DO NOT FILE** — This form for individually terminated employees. These employees are to be included at year end with all other employees.

6. **ACCEPTABLE FORMS** — The DE43/DE 43A may be accompanied by either the paper W-2's/W-2P's or magnetic tape. Submission via magnetic tape requires prior approval of format by Department of Benefit Payments, P.O. Box 105, Sacramento, California 95801.

7. **SEPARATION OF FORMS** — When mailing Forms DE 43/DE 43A and W-2's/W-2P's, please separate from other forms being filed with Department of Benefit Payments (DBP). Do not mail Franchise Tax Board and Internal Revenue forms to DBP.

8. **OPTIONAL FILING PROCEDURES** — See Form DE 44 (Employer's Tax Guide) Par. 19.

9. **MAILING** — Mail forms and packages by First Class Mail. Do not mail with other documents. Mail to P.O. Box 105, Sacramento, California 95801. If you need further instructions, please refer to Form DE 44, Par. 20.

---

1 Control number	222	2 Employer's State number **190 8847**	

3 Employer's name, address, and ZIP code	4 Subtotal ☐ Correction ☐ Void ☐		
HAZEL HAYWORTH DBA/HAZEL'S BOUTIQUE 921 HAYWOOD DR. SANTA CRUZ, CA 95062	5 Employer's identification number **94-7341691**		
	6 Advance EIC payment	7	

8 Employee's social security number **541-42-7361**	9 Federal income tax withheld **164.30**	10 Wages, tips, other compensation **2,120.00**	11 FICA tax withheld **159.20**	12 Total FICA wages **2,120.00**
13 Employee's name (first, middle, last) and address **MARY LOUISE WILSON 1812 FRONT STREET SANTA CRUZ, CA 95060**	14 Pension plan coverage? Yes/No **NO**	15	16 FICA tips	
	18 State income tax withheld **12.50**	19 State wages, tips, etc. **2,120.00**	20 Name of state **CALIFORNIA**	
	21 Local income tax withheld	22 Local wages, tips, etc.	23 Name of locality	

Copy 1 For State, City, or Local Tax Department
Employee's and employer's copy compared. ☐

Wage and Tax Statement

The W-2 form is a report to the Internal Revenue Service and your State Franchise Tax Board, or other tax-collecting agency, as to the amount of earnings you had during the year, the amount of income tax withheld, and the other benefit contributions deducted from the employee's wages.

The forms consists of five parts (or separate sheets) which can be torn apart with copies to be mailed to:

Copy A is for the Internal Revenue Service and must be mailed to the service center serving your area. It is usually mailed in with the quarter's tax return. Be sure to attach the transmittal form.

Copy 1 is for the state and mailed to the agency with the transmittal and tax return.

Copy B is part of the group given to the employee, and is to be attached to his/her state income tax return.

Copy C is to be retained by the wage earner and attached to his/her own copy of the income tax return.

Copy 2 is for the employee to attach to his/her state income tax return, so that the state can see the amount of wages earned, the withholding, etc.

Copy D is for the employer. File it in the same folder that contains your quarterly reports.

After preparing the W-2 forms, if there are a number of them, run an adding machine tape and attach the tape to the Reconciliation Transmittal Form which the IRS will send you. It is similar to the state form illustrated on page 111. Even if there is only one W-2 form to be mailed, the transmittal form must accompany it.

Now that you have looked at the W-2 wage-report form and know what it is for, let's fill it out with the information we have on the employee-compensation sheet. (All of the quarterly forms are prepared from this information. If the bookkeeper is careful and checks the work as it progresses, the figures at the end of the year will be accurate and will present no problem in making up the forms. If there is more than one employee, recap the figures on a columnar pad similar to the compensation sheet by posting the names of all the employees, along with the totals of their individual sheets, then add them up.)

At the end of the year, the IRS will send the employer a booklet which contains the trasmittal sheet and a number of W-2 forms. These are set up the same as the commercial forms which are purchased at the office supply store. I have found the commercially printed forms to be better. They contain carbons of a non-carbon type, and come in sheets of five each. The paper is lighter than the kind furnished by the IRS, and the last copy is more readable. If you prefer to use the IRS copies, they are filled out in the same manner as the example.

The first information to type on the W-2 form is the Proprietor's name, the name of the business, the address of the business, and the federal withholding number. (See illustration.)

The next information required is the employer's state withholding number. This will be found on the state quarterly return. This number is the purpose of filling out the application to the state for an employer number. It is the number of the account which will be set up by the collection office.

Below the employer's name, enter the employee's social security number. In Block 9, enter the employee's income tax withheld; in this case the figure is $153.11. (The form may vary from year to year. It seldom seems to be set up the same way for two years in a row. If you learn to fill them out, you will know what to look for regardless of the sequence of amounts needed.)

In space 10, enter the gross wages, tips, etc.

In space 11, the amount of FICA withheld ($159.20) is entered.

Space 12 is for the total FICA wages. (This could be less than total wages. If the employee earned $47,000 in the year, the FICA wages would be $45,000; the maximum of taxable FICA wages.)

Space 14 asks if the employee were covered by a qualified pension plan. In large companies, this would be answered with a "yes." Hazel has no such plan, so the answer is "no."

Spaces 15 and 16 are blank, but could be used to show the amount of excludable sick pay the employee received. Sick pay is deductible.

In space 18, the state or local tax ($12.50) is entered.

Space 19 is for state and local wages. Some employees might work in more than one state during the year and could have state income tax withheld from each of them. This box is to show the amount earned in each state, the withholding, and the state for which it was withheld.

In the "name" box, type in the name of the employee, with the home address. This finishes the W-2 form, and they can now be segregated.

The first two copies and the bottom copy stay with the employer (Copy A, Copy 1, and Copy D), while the third, fourth, and fifth (Copy B, Copy C, and Copy 2) are given to the employee. Be sure to mail the copies. Then you can forget about them until the end of next year.

State Sales Tax Return

The state sales tax return can be either a monthly or a quarterly tax return. It depends on the type of business and the amount of sales tax collected. When you apply for your resale number, the tax people will inform you of your status. The resale number is proof that you have been approved to collect sales tax. The number will be requested by every company who sells you merchandise without adding the tax.

The sales tax form should be prepared from the ledger figures so that all merchandise sold will be included in the amount used. There could be sales that are not included on the daily sales sheet, but would be included in the sales figures in the ledger.

In preparing this sales tax return, the figures have been arbitrarily selected to serve as an example only. Also, the form shown is from California. Again, the one for your state may be different. But if you follow the procedure as given, filling out your state's return will be that much easier. Usually the form, which can be prepared either monthly or quarterly, comes printed with the owner's name, address, and dates, eliminating the need to write anything in those spaces.

Line 1. Total Sales. $12,547.43

Line 2. Purchase price of tangible personal property purchased without paying California sales or use tax that was used for some other purpose than resale. (Personal property is inventory.) This could be merchandise taken out of stock for the personal use of the owner. Example: a chain saw used by the owner of a hardware store or a dress taken out of stock by Hazel for her own use. She hasn't paid sales tax to the distributor because the dress was originally for resale. The tax people don't want to lose the tax even on a $19.95 dress, so Hazel would have to enter that amount on this line, and add it to the gross sales. That way, she would be paying tax on it to the collecting agency. (In this case, she could enter her own cost price, rather than her retail value.)

Line 3. Total of lines 1 & 2. This is the amount on which sales tax is paid, unless there are deductions.

Line 4. Sales to other retailers. This happens often in the drug-store/pharmacy-type business. Sometimes the store is out of a particular drug which the customer needs right away. Druggists often have a working agreement with other stores to furnish what is needed. If our store sold a drug to the store down the street, it would be without the tax included. The amount would be entered here.

Line 5. Sales of food products for human consumption. This is for the small grocery store type of business that sells food and notions. The amount of food for human consumption would be entered here. Everything else would be taxable. If in doubt, check with your state collecting agency. A record of the various kinds of sales would have to be kept either by cash register or by sales slips.

Line 6. Non-taxable labor. This could be for a shop that sells parts and repairs, and would include vacuum cleaner shops, auto repair garages, body shops, etc.

Line 7. Amount of sales tax included in the figure on Line 1. Zero

Line 9. The total of all the amounts on Lines 4 through 8. Zero

Line 10. Amount on which State and County (in California) sales tax will be collected. This is Line 3 less Line 9, or $12,547.43.

Line 11. Amount of tax on above amount at 5% of figure. In our case, it is $627.37.

Line 12. Amount on which state tax applies. This is the same as Line 10, $12,547.43.

Line 14. Total Lines 12 and 13. Our example shows $12,547.43.

Line 16. Amount on which local tax applies. Some counties and cities have their own sales tax which is paid to the state and forwarded on to the city or county. Our answer is, again, $12,547.43.

Line 17. Amount of local tax. 1% times figure. Ours is $125.47.

Line 19. Total state, county, local, and district tax. Ours is $752.84.

Line 20. This is for out-of-state purchases on which the buyer had to pay tax. It wouldn't apply to small shop owners in most cases. If it should occur, check with your local collecting agency as to what *their procedure* might be.

Lines 21 through 25 are all the same figure, since none of the tax collected has been remitted to the collecting agency. If monthly deposits had been made, the amount of those deposits would go into these two boxes. The difference between the total of the two and the total amount of tax would be the amount of money due the agency.

Remember to sign and return the form with your check enclosed. Examine the form as filled in on the following page and follow the steps I have described. The procedure is not as complicated as it seems, and shouldn't be difficult to follow.

3T-401-AC2 (S1&2F) REV. 8 (11-75)

STATE OF CALIFORNIA
BOARD OF EQUALIZATION – Department of Business Taxes

STATE, LOCAL and DISTRICT SALES and USE TAX RETURN

DUE ON OR BEFORE: OCTOBER 31, 19		FOR 4TH QUARTER, 19___ PERIOD YEAR

Mail to:

STATE BOARD OF EQUALIZATION
P. O. BOX 1799
SACRAMENTO, CA 95808

PARTIAL PERIOD

BUSINESS CODE	AREA CODE	ACCOUNT NUMBER
		496-873 9593

NAME
HAZEL'S BOUTIQUE

BUSINESS ADDRESS
921 HAYWOOD DRIVE

CITY
SANTA CRUZ, CA 95062

REPORTING BASIS
QUARTERLY

READ INSTRUCTIONS BEFORE PREPARING

STATE SALES AND USE TAX

1. TOTAL SALES ___ IF YOU INCLUDE TAX CHARGED – SEE LINE 7		$ 12,547.43
2. ADD–Purchase price of tangible personal property purchased without California sales or use tax and used for some purpose other than resale ENTER "NONE" IF YOU HAVE NOTHING TO REPORT		–O–
3. TOTAL (Line 1 plus Line 2) ___ ENTER "NONE" IF YOU HAVE NOTHING TO REPORT		$ 12,547.43
DEDUCT EXEMPT TRANSACTIONS	$	
4. Sales to other retailers for purposes of resale		
5. Sales of food products for human consumption		
6. Nontaxable labor (Repair, Installation, etc.)		
7. Amount of sales tax (if any) included in Line 1	–O–	
8. Other exempt transactions (See instruction 8)		
9. TOTAL TRANSACTIONS EXEMPT FROM STATE & COUNTY SALES & USE TAX (Lines 4 thru 8)		–O–
10. Amount on which STATE & COUNTY Sales and Use Tax applies (Line 3 minus Line 9)		$ 12,547.43
11. AMOUNT OF TAX ___ 5% (4¾% State, ¼% County) (Multiply amount on Line 10 by .05)		$ 627.37

UNIFORM LOCAL SALES AND USE TAX

12. Amount on which State Tax applies (Enter amount from Line 10)	$ 12,547.43
13. ADD–Other local tax adjustments (See instruction 13)	–O–
14. TOTAL (Line 12 plus Line 13)	$ 12,547.43
15. DEDUCT–Transactions exempt from local sales and use tax only (See instruction 15)	–O–
16. Amount on which LOCAL Tax applies (Line 14 minus Line 15)	$ 12,547.43
17. AMOUNT OF LOCAL TAX 1% (Multiply amount on Line 16 by .01)	$ 125.47

DISTRICT SALES AND USE TAX

18. Amount of San Francisco Bay Area Rapid Transit District Tax (From Line A9 Column A of Schedule A)	$ –O–

TOTAL TAX

19. TOTAL STATE, COUNTY, LOCAL & DISTRICT TAX (Total of Lines 11, 17 & 18) TOTAL TAX HERE		$ 752.84
20. Deduct amount of sales or use tax or reimbursement therefor imposed by other states and paid by you on the purchase of tangible personal property. Purchase price must be included in Line 2. (See Instruction 20)		–O–
21. NET STATE, COUNTY, LOCAL AND DISTRICT TAX (Line 19 minus Line 20)		$ 752.84
22. LESS–Tax Prepayments 1ST MONTH 2ND MONTH Total Prepayments		–O–
23. REMAINING STATE COUNTY, LOCAL AND DISTRICT TAX (Line 21 minus Line 22)		$ 752.84
24. Penalty of 10% (.10) plus interest at 1% (.01) per month or part of a month must be added unless payment is made on or before the due date shown above.	Penalty	–O–
	Interest	–O–
25. TOTAL AMOUNT DUE AND PAYABLE (Line 23 plus Line 24)		$ 752.84

REPORT OF MOTOR VEHICLE FUEL (GASOLINE)

COMPLETE ONLY FOR GASOLINE TRANSACTIONS Amount included in Line 10 for gasoline sold and used	$
Number of Gallons sold and used	

I hereby certify that this return, including any accompanying schedules and statements, has been examined by me and to the best of my knowledge and belief is a true, correct and complete return.

SIGNATURE
TITLE   *Hazel Hayworth*   OWNER

DUMMY RETURN

The Purpose of It All

Delving into the theories of accounting can be either very pleasurable or exceedingly boring. It all depends on the outlook of the party involved. The degree of complexity in the accounting system used depends on the growth of the business, the amount of information needed in order to administer the operations and to satisfy Uncle Sam that you are paying the proper amount of taxes on your earnings. If it weren't for the Internal Revenue Service, the business operator would need know only how much his/her gross sales were, how much the expenses and costs of materials were, and the balance not paid out would be his. (Profit.)

Uncle Sam insists that the shopowner do a bit more than that, feeling that along the line somewhere the owner might filch a dollar or two. The government requests that you show where every dollar of the sales income goes in order to calculate what the owner owes the government in the form of taxes. For this reason, it is necessary to have a number of headings under which to post the sales, purchases, and expenses so that the "Great Collecting Father" will know we are honest and willing to support his high style of living.

Below is a typical Income Statement for the smaller business. Using it, we will examine the various accounts to see how the IRS might view them.

Hazel's Gift Shop & Boutique
Santa Cruz, California

Income Statement: January 1, 19____ to December 31, 19____

			%
Gross Sales		$58,982.75	100.0
Less: Returns by Customers		986.50	1.7
Net Sales		57,996.25	98.3
Less Cost of Sales:			
Inventory, January 1, 19____	$11,765.42		19.9
Merchandise Purchased	22,031.60		37.3
Merchandise Available	33,797.02		57.3
Inventory,			
December 31, 19____	12,265.20		20.8
Cost of Sales		$21,531.82	36.5
Gross Profit on Sales		$36,464.43	61.8
Operating Expenses:			
Advertising	$ 7,130.00		12.0
Bad Debt Expense	802.50		1.3
Car and Truck Expense	425.25		.7
Depreciation	660.60		1.1
Dues and Subscriptions	125.00		.2

Insurance	3,600.00	6.1
Interest	595.00	1.0
Legal and Professional	600.00	1.0
Office Expense	219.29	.4
Rent	4,200.00	7.1
Repairs and Maintenance	319.29	.5
Supplies	710.94	1.2
Taxes	947.70	1.6
Telephone	720.29	1.2
Travel and Entertainment	403.00	.7
Utilities	2,655.25	4.5
Wages	2,120.00	3.6
Outside Labor	250.00	.4
Miscellaneous	188.43	.3

Total Operating Expenses	$26,672.54	45.2
Net Profit from Operations	$ 9,791.89	16.6

Other Income:

Discounts on Purchases	$ 210.95	.3
Sublet Floor Space	1,200.00	2.0
Total Other Income	$ 1,410.95	2.3
Net Profit for the Year	$11,202.84	19.0

One of the first things a person thinks of when starting a new business is, "Oh, boy! Now I can do anything I want, have anything I want, and go anywhere I want, and charge it all to the business!"

Don't believe it.

The Internal Revenue Service has some very snoopy people on its payroll who have been trained to look at income statements for figures that don't belong. How much additional money they can take in on "tax audits" is the criterion of how far they may go in the system. You can bet those fellows and ladies want to go f-a-a-a-r.

How to Know Where You Stand

The Internal Revenue Service also compiles records of various types of businesses, and the percentages of expenses in each type of business. If your return shows anything too high, the computer will kick it out and you are in for an audit. At any rate, if you don't get an audit within the first or second year, you will certainly get one the third or fourth. This harks back to the basis that a business doesn't usually make money the first two or three years, but if expenses are still too *high,* you might wake up some morning with the little man in thick glasses and fat briefcase sitting in your lap. When such a thing happens, be certain you have all of your records filed in a manner that they will be easy to find.

What will the little man in thick glasses look for?

What An Auditor Looks For

The first thing an auditor will look at will be the gross sales, how the figures were obtained, and how the records are kept. Sale slips should be totaled, filed, and posted daily to the sales journal.

After inspecting the sales slips, the auditor then might delve into the bank statements to determine if the money received from sales was all deposited in the checking account. If there should be a larger amount of deposit than the amount of gross sales, he might inquire where the extra money came from, and search the records for same. He could also suspect that the owner had some cash (folding money) sales and didn't enter them on the journal.

Next, the auditor, being trained in suspicion, might inspect your invoice ledger, checking the amount of merchandise purchased against the amount of gross sales. He might even calculate what your gross sales should have been by adding the national average of mark-up to your purchases (minus your inventory at the end of the year) and see if it compares with your actual figures. If it doesn't, he will ask questions.

The auditor will want to see the invoices, receipts for cash purchases, out-of-pocket or by check, to determine if they are legitimate purchases and not funds taken from the business for personal use. He will want to inspect the cash fund records, making certain that all cash disbursements are proper. He will possibly examine the cancelled checks if there is any suspicion of illegal dealings. The best system is one which does not pose other questions to an auditor but answers questions right up front.

If the owner does not have an auditable accounting system, he will be levied a fine and compelled to have one installed. It is much better to start your system from the very beginning of the business, and let it grow as the business grows. There are hundreds of account titles and headings which can be used, but using more than is necessary for your own business is a waste of valuable time. Keep only those that are necessary.

I have partially filled out the following sample of the 1040 Federal Income Tax form so you can trace the figures from the Income Statement on page 118. I do want to point out, however, that there are a number of items that are deductible which I have not included in the income statement or on the tax form. You may have clothing, entertainment, and in some cases, office-in-the-home expenses to be included. These are all legitimate if you can show that such items were incurred in the line of business.

Take a good look at the tax form and the Schedule C income statement, and then we'll talk about other deductibles.

Form **1040**	Department of the Treasury—Internal Revenue Service		
	U.S. Individual Income Tax Return 19	(0)	

For the year January 1-December 31, 19 , or other tax year beginning , 19 , ending , 19 . OMB No. 1545-0074

Use IRS label. Otherwise, please print or type.	Your first name and initial (if joint return, also give spouse's name and initial)	Last name	Your social security number
	HAZEL E.	HAYWORTH	441 36 8734
	Present home address (Number and street, including apartment number, or rural route)		Spouse's social security number
	376 MAIN ST. APT. H-4		
	City, town or post office, State, and ZIP code	Your occupation	RETAIL SALES
	SANTA CRUZ, CALIFORNIA 95060	Spouse's occupation	

Presidential Election Campaign ▶ Do you want $1 to go to this fund? ☒ Yes ☐ No   **Note:** Checking "Yes" will not increase your tax or reduce your refund.
If joint return, does your spouse want $1 to go to this fund? ☐ Yes ☐ No

For Privacy Act and Paperwork Reduction Act Notice, see Instructions.

Filing Status

Check only one box.

1 ☒ Single
2 ☐ Married filing joint return (even if only one had income)
3 ☐ Married filing separate return. Enter spouse's social security no. above and full name here. _____
4 ☐ Head of household (with qualifying person). (See page 6 of Instructions.) If the qualifying person is your unmarried child but not your dependent, write child's name here. _____
5 ☐ Qualifying widow(er) with dependent child (Year spouse died ▶ 19). (See page 6 of Instructions.)

Exemptions

Always check the box labeled Yourself. Check other boxes if they apply.

6a ☒ Yourself	☐ 65 or over	☐ Blind	Enter number of boxes checked on 6a and b ▶
b ☐ Spouse	☐ 65 or over	☐ Blind	

c First names of your dependent children who lived with you _____ } Enter number of children listed on 6c ▶

d Other dependents: (1) Name	(2) Relationship	(3) Number of months lived in your home	(4) Did dependent have income of $1,000 or more?	(5) Did you provide more than one-half of dependent's support?

Enter number of other dependents ▶

e Total number of exemptions claimed . . . .   Add numbers entered in boxes above ▶

Income

Please attach Copy B of your Forms W-2, W-2G, and W-2P here.

If you do not have a W-2, see page 5 of Instructions.

7	Wages, salaries, tips, etc.	7	
8	Interest income (also attach Schedule B if over $400 or you have any All-Savers interest) . . .	8	
9a	Dividends (also attach Schedule B if over $400) _____ , 9b Exclusion _____		
c	Subtract line 9b from line 9a and enter the result	9c	
10	Refunds of State and local income taxes, from worksheet on page 10 of Instructions (do not enter an amount unless you deducted those taxes in an earlier year—see page 10 of Instructions)	10	
11	Alimony received	11	
12	Business income or (loss) (attach Schedule C) . . . . ▶	12	
13	Capital gain or (loss) (attach Schedule D)	13	
14	40% capital gain distributions not reported on line 13 (See page 10 of Instructions)	14	
15	Supplemental gains or (losses) (attach Form 4797)	15	
16	Fully taxable pensions, IRA distributions, and annuities not reported on line 17	16	
17a	Other pensions and annuities, including rollovers. Total received 17a _____		
b	Taxable amount, if any, from worksheet on page 10 of Instructions	17b	
18	Rents, royalties, partnerships, estates, trusts, etc. (attach Schedule E)	18	
19	Farm income or (loss) (attach Schedule F) . . . . ▶	19	
20a	Unemployment compensation (insurance). Total received 20a _____		
b	Taxable amount, if any, from worksheet on page 11 of Instructions	20b	
21	Other income (state nature and source—see page 11 of Instructions) _____		
		21	
22	**Total income.** Add amounts in column for lines 7 through 21 . . . . ▶	22	

Please attach check or money order here.

Adjustments to Income

(See Instructions on page 11)

23	Moving expense (attach Form 3903 or 3903F)	23		
24	Employee business expenses (attach Form 2106)	24		
25a	IRA deduction, from the worksheet on page 12	25a		
b	Enter here IRA payments you made in 1984 that are included in line 25a above ▶ _____			
26	Payments to a Keogh (H.R. 10) retirement plan	26		
27	Penalty on early withdrawal of savings	27		
28	Alimony paid	28		
29	Deduction for a married couple when both work (attach Schedule W)	29		
30	Disability income exclusion (attach Form 2440)	30		
31	**Total adjustments.** Add lines 23 through 30 . . . . ▶		31	

Adjusted Gross Income

32	**Adjusted gross income.** Subtract line 31 from line 22. If this line is less than $10,000, see "Earned Income Credit" (line 59) on page 16 of Instructions. If you want IRS to figure your tax, see page 3 of Instructions . . . . ▶	32	

Form 1040 (19   )

Page **2**

Tax Compu-tation (See Instructions on page 13)	33	Amount from line 32 (adjusted gross income)	**33**	
	34a	If you itemize, complete Schedule A (Form 1040) and enter the amount from Schedule A, line 28	**34a**	
		Caution: If you have unearned income and can be claimed as a dependent on your parent's return, check here ▶ ☐ and see page 13 of the Instructions. Also see page 13 of the Instructions if: • You are married filing a separate return and your spouse itemizes deductions, OR • You file Form 4563, OR • You are a dual-status alien.		
	34b	If you do not itemize deductions on Schedule A (Form 1040), complete the worksheet on page 14. Then enter the allowable part of your charitable contributions here	**34b**	
	35	Subtract line 34a or 34b, whichever applies, from line 33	**35**	
	36	Multiply $1,000 by the total number of exemptions claimed on Form 1040, line 6e	**36**	
	37	Taxable Income. Subtract line 36 from line 35	**37**	
	38	Tax. Enter tax here and check if from ☐ Tax Table, ☐ Tax Rate Schedule X, Y, or Z, or ☐ Schedule G	**38**	
	39	Additional Taxes. (See page 14 of Instructions.) Enter here and check if from ☐ Form 4970, ☐ Form 4972, ☐ Form 5544, or ☐ section 72 penalty taxes	**39**	
	40	**Total.** Add lines 38 and 39 . . . . ▶	**40**	

Credits (See Instructions on page 14)	41	Credit for the elderly (attach Schedules R&RP)	**41**	
	42	Foreign tax credit (attach Form 1116)	**42**	
	43	Investment credit (attach Form 3468)	**43**	
	44	Partial credit for political contributions	**44**	
	45	Credit for child and dependent care expenses (attach Form 2441)	**45**	
	46	Jobs credit (attach Form 5884)	**46**	
	47	Residential energy credit (attach Form 5695)	**47**	
	48	**Total credits.** Add lines 41 through 47		**48**
	49	**Balance.** Subtract line 48 from line 40 and enter difference (but not less than zero) . . . . ▶		**49**

Other Taxes (Including Advance EIC Payments)	50	Self-employment tax (attach Schedule SE)	**50**	
	51	Alternative minimum tax (attach Form 6251)	**51**	
	52	Tax from recapture of investment credit (attach Form 4255)	**52**	
	53	Social security tax on tip income not reported to employer (attach Form 4137)	**53**	
	54	Uncollected employee social security tax and RRTA tax on tips (from Form W-2)	**54**	
	55	Tax on an IRA (attach Form 5329)	**55**	
06	56	**Total tax.** Add lines 49 through 55 . . . . ▶	**56**	

Payments Attach Forms W-2, W-2G, and W-2P to front.	57	Federal income tax withheld	**57**	
	58	1983 estimated tax payments and amount applied from 1982 return	**58**	
	59	Earned income credit. If line 33 is under $10,000, see page 16 . .	**59**	
	60	Amount paid with Form 4868	**60**	
	61	Excess social security tax and RRTA tax withheld (two or more employers)	**61**	
	62	Credit for Federal tax on special fuels and oils (attach Form 4136)	**62**	
	63	Regulated Investment Company credit (attach Form 2439)	**63**	
	64	**Total payments.** Add lines 57 through 63 . . . . ▶		**64**

Refund or Amount You Owe	65	If line 64 is larger than line 56, enter amount **OVERPAID** . . . . ▶	**65**	
	66	Amount of line 65 to be **REFUNDED TO YOU** . . . . ▶	**66**	
	67	Amount of line 65 to be applied to your 1984 estimated tax . . . . . ▶	**67**	
	68	If line 56 is larger than line 64, enter **AMOUNT YOU OWE.** Attach check or money order for full amount payable to "Internal Revenue Service." Write your social security number and "1983 Form 1040" on it . . . . ▶	**68**	
		(Check ▶ ☐ if Form 2210 (2210F) is attached. See page 17 of Instructions.) $		

Please Sign Here

Under penalties of perjury, I declare that I have examined this return and accompanying schedules and statements, and to the best of my knowledge and belief, they are true, correct, and complete. Declaration of preparer (other than taxpayer) is based on all information of which preparer has any knowledge.

▶ _____ _____ ▶ _____
Your signature   Date   Spouse's signature (if filing jointly, BOTH must sign)

Paid Preparer's Use Only	Preparer's signature ▶	Date	Check if self-employed ☐	Preparer's social security no.
	Firm's name (or yours, if self-employed) ▶ and address		E.I. No.	
			ZIP code	

☆ U.S. GOVERNMENT PRINTING OFFICE 19   390-068   E.I. #52-1074467

SCHEDULE C
(Form 1040)

Department of the Treasury
Internal Revenue Service (0)

Profit or (Loss) From Business or Profession
(Sole Proprietorship)
Partnerships, Joint Ventures, etc., Must File Form 1065.
▶ **Attach to Form 1040 or Form 1041.** ▶ **See Instructions for Schedule C (Form 1040).**

OMB No. 1545-0074

19
09

Name of proprietor

Social security number of proprietor

A Main business activity (see Instructions) ▶ _____ ; product ▶ _____

B Business name and address ▶ ....

C Employer identification number

D Method(s) used to value closing inventory:
  (1) ☐ Cost   **(2)** ☐ Lower of cost or market   **(3)** ☐ Other (attach explanation)

E Accounting method: **(1)** ☐ Cash   **(2)** ☐ Accrual   **(3)** ☐ Other (specify) ▶ ....

	Yes	No

F Was there any major change in determining quantities, costs, or valuations between opening and closing inventory? . . . . . .
  If "Yes," attach explanation.

G Did you deduct expenses for an office in your home? . . . .

PART I.—Income

1 **a** Gross receipts or sales	**1a**	
b Less: Returns and allowances	**1b**	
c Subtract line 1b from line 1a and enter the balance here	**1c**	
2 Cost of goods sold and/or operations (Part III, line 8)	**2**	
3 Subtract line 2 from line 1c and enter the **gross profit** here .	**3**	
4 **a** Windfall Profit Tax Credit or Refund received in 1983 (see Instructions)	**4a**	
b Other income	**4b**	
5 Add lines 3, 4a, and 4b. This is the **gross income** . . . . ▶	**5**	

PART II.—Deductions

6 Advertising		**23** Repairs		
7 Bad debts from sales or services (Cash		**24** Supplies (not included in Part III) . .		
method taxpayers, see Instructions) . .		**25** Taxes (Do not include Windfall		
8 Bank service charges		Profit Tax here. See line 29.) . . .		
9 Car and truck expenses		**26** Travel and entertainment . . .		
10 Commissions		**27** Utilities and telephone		
11 Depletion		**28** **a** Wages		
12 Depreciation and Section 179 deduction		**b** Jobs credit		
from Form 4562 (not included in Part		**c** Subtract line 28b from 28a . .		
III)		**29** Windfall Profit Tax withheld in 1983		
13 Dues and publications		**30** Other expenses (specify):		
14 Employee benefit programs . . .		**a**		
15 Freight (not included in Part III) . .		**b**		
16 Insurance		**c**		
17 Interest on business indebtedness . .		**d**		
18 Laundry and cleaning		**e**		
19 Legal and professional services . .		**f**		
20 Office expense		**g**		
21 Pension and profit-sharing plans . .		**h**		
22 Rent on business property		**i**		

31 Add amounts in columns for lines 6 through 30i. These are the **total deductions** . . . . ▶	**31**	

32 Net profit or (loss). Subtract line 31 from line 5 and enter the result. If a profit, enter on Form 1040, line 12, and on Schedule SE, Part I, line 2 (or Form 1041, line 6). If a loss, go on to line 33 . . . . | **32** |

33 If you have a loss, you must answer this question: "Do you have amounts for which you are not at risk in this business (see Instructions)?" ☐ Yes ☐ No
If "Yes," you must attach Form 6198. If "No," enter the loss on Form 1040, line 12, and on Schedule SE, Part I, line 2 (or Form 1041, line 6).

PART III.—Cost of Goods Sold and/or Operations (See Schedule C Instructions for Part III)

1 Inventory at beginning of year (if different from last year's closing inventory, attach explanation)	**1**	
2 Purchases less cost of items withdrawn for personal use	**2**	
3 Cost of labor (do not include salary paid to yourself)	**3**	
4 Materials and supplies	**4**	
5 Other costs	**5**	
6 Add lines 1 through 5	**6**	
7 Less: Inventory at end of year	**7**	
8 **Cost of goods sold and/or operations.** Subtract line 7 from line 6. Enter here and in Part I, line 2, above. . .	**8**	

For Paperwork Reduction Act Notice, see Form 1040 Instructions.

Schedule C (Form 1040) 19

✿ U.S. G.P.O. 19 −390−080 E.I. 43⁻0787287

This page was purposely left blank.

SCHEDULES A&B
(Form 1040)
Department of the Treasury
Internal Revenue Service   (0)

Schedule A—Itemized Deductions
(Schedule B is on back)
▶ Attach to Form 1040. ▶ See Instructions for Schedules A and B (Form 1040).

OMB No. 1545-0074
19 07

Name(s) as shown on Form 1040 | Your social security number

Medical and Dental Expenses (Do not include expenses reimbursed or paid by others.) (See page 18 of Instructions.)	**1** Medicines and drugs	**1**		
	2 Write 1% of Form 1040, line 33	**2**		
	3 Subtract line 2 from line 1. If line 2 is more than line 1, write zero . .		**3**	
	4 Other medical and dental expenses:			
	a Doctors, dentists, nurses, hospitals, insurance premiums you paid for medical and dental care, etc.	**4a**		
	b Transportation	**4b**		
	c Other (list—include hearing aids, dentures, eyeglasses, etc.) ▶...	**4c**		
	5 Add lines 3 through 4c		**5**	
	6 Multiply amount on Form 1040, line 33, by 5% (.05)		**6**	
	7 Subtract line 6 from line 5. If line 6 is more than line 5, write zero . . . . ▶		**7**	
Taxes (See page 19 of Instructions.)	**8** State and local income	**8**		
	9 Real estate	**9**		
	10 a General sales (see sales tax tables)	**10a**		
	b General sales on motor vehicles	**10b**		
	11 Other (list—include personal property) ▶..................................	**11**		
	12 Add lines 8 through 11. Write your answer here . . . . ▶		**12**	
Interest Expense (See page 20 of Instructions.)	**13 a** Home mortgage interest paid to financial institutions	**13a**		
	b Home mortgage interest paid to individuals (show that person's name and address) ▶..	**13b**		
	14 Credit cards and charge accounts	**14**		
	15 Other (list) ▶..	**15**		
	16 Add lines 13a through 15. Write your answer here . . . . ▶		**16**	
Contributions (See page 20 of Instructions.)	**17 a** Cash contributions. (If you gave $3,000 or more to any one organization, report those contributions on line 17b.)	**17a**		
	b Cash contributions totaling $3,000 or more to any one organization. (Show to whom you gave and how much you gave.) ▶.........	**17b**		
	18 Other than cash (attach required statement)	**18**		
	19 Carryover from prior year	**19**		
	20 Add lines 17a through 19. Write your answer here . . . . ▶		**20**	
Casualty and Theft Losses	**21** Total casualty or theft loss(es) (attach Form 4684) (see page 20 of Instructions). . . . . . ▶		**21**	
Miscellaneous Deductions (See page 21 of Instructions.)	**22** Union and professional dues	**22**		
	23 Tax return preparation fee	**23**		
	24 Other (list) ▶...	**24**		
	25 Add lines 22 through 24. Write your answer here . . . . ▶		**25**	
Summary of Itemized Deductions (See page 21 of Instructions.)	**26** Add lines 7, 12, 16, 20, 21, and 25		**26**	
	27 If you checked Form 1040 { Filing Status box 2 or 5, write $3,400 / Filing Status box 1 or 4, write $2,300 / Filing Status box 3, write $1,700 }		**27**	
	28 Subtract line 27 from line 26. Write your answer here and on Form 1040, line 34a. (If line 27 is more than line 26, see the Instructions for line 28 on page 21.) . . . . ▶		**28**	

For Paperwork Reduction Act Notice, see Form 1040 Instructions.

Schedule A (Form 1040) 19

Schedules A&B (Form 1040) 19

Schedule B—Interest and Dividend Income 08   OMB No. 1545-0074   Page **2**

Name(s) as shown on Form 1040 (Do not enter name and social security number if shown on other side) | Your social security number

Part I
Interest Income

(See pages 9 and 21 of Instructions.)

Also complete Part III.

If you received more than $400 in interest or you received any interest from an All-Savers Certificate, you must complete Part I and list ALL interest received. If you received interest as a nominee for another, or you received or paid accrued interest on securities transferred between interest payment dates, see page 22.

Interest income other than interest from All-Savers Certificates	Amount
1 Interest income from seller-financed mortgages. (See Instructions and show name of payer.) ▶ **1**	
2 Other interest income (list name of payer) ▶	
....	
2	
3 Add lines 1 and 2 .... **3**	

Interest from All-Savers Certificates (ASCs). (See page 22.)	Amount
4 .... **4**	
5 Add amounts on line 4 .... **5**	
6 Write the amount of your ASC exclusion from the worksheet on page 22 of Instructions . **6**	
7 Subtract line 6 from line 5 .... **7**	
8 Add lines 3 and 7. Write your answer here and on Form 1040, line 8 ...... ▶ **8**	

Part II
Dividend Income

(See pages 9 and 22 of Instructions.)

Also complete Part III.

If you received more than $400 in gross dividends (including capital gain distributions) and other distributions on stock, or you are electing to exclude qualified reinvested dividends from a public utility, complete Part II. If you received dividends as a nominee for another, see page 22.

Name of payer	Amount
9	
9	
10 Add amounts on line 9 .... **10**	
11 Capital gain distributions. Enter here and on line 15, Schedule D.* **11**	
12 Nontaxable distributions. (See Instructions for adjustment to basis.) **12**	
13 Exclusion of qualified reinvested dividends from a public utility. (See page 22 of Instructions.) **13**	
14 Add lines 11, 12, and 13 .... **14**	
15 Subtract line 14 from line 10. Write your answer here and on Form 1040, line 9a . . ▶ **15**	

If you received capital gain distributions for the year and you do not need Schedule D to report any other gains or losses, do not file that schedule. Instead, enter 40% of your capital gain distributions on Form 1040, line 14.

Part III
Foreign Accounts and Foreign Trusts

(See page 22 of Instructions.)

If you received more than $400 of interest or dividends, OR if you had a foreign account or were a grantor of, or a transferor to, a foreign trust, you must answer both questions in Part III. | Yes | No

16 At any time during the tax year, did you have an interest in or a signature or other authority over a bank account, securities account, or other financial account in a foreign country? (See page 23 of the instructions for exceptions and filing requirements for Form 90-22.1.) ....

If "Yes," write the name of the foreign country ▶ ....

17 Were you the grantor of, or transferor to, a foreign trust which existed during the current tax year, whether or not you have any beneficial interest in it? If "Yes," you may have to file Forms 3520, 3520-A, or 926 ....

For Paperwork Reduction Act Notice, see Form 1040 Instructions.   Schedule B (Form 1040) 19

☆ U.S. GOVERNMENT PRINTING OFFICE: 19' –390-076   23-188-5979

This page was purposely left blank.

Form **W-4** (Rev. January 1984)	Department of the Treasury—Internal Revenue Service **Employee's Withholding Allowance Certificate**	OMB No. 1545-0010

1 Type or print your full name	2 Your social security number

Home address (number and street or rural route) City or town, State, and ZIP code	3 Marital Status	☐ Single ☐ Married ☐ Married, but withhold at higher Single rate **Note:** If married, but legally separated, or spouse is a nonresident alien, check the Single box.

4 Total number of allowances you are claiming (from line F of the worksheet on page 2) . . . . . .

5 Additional amount, if any, you want deducted from each pay . . . . $

6 I claim exemption from withholding because (see instructions and check boxes below that apply):

  a ☐ Last year I did not owe any Federal income tax and had a right to a full refund of **ALL** income tax withheld, **AND**

  b ☐ This year I do not expect to owe any Federal income tax and expect to have a right to a full refund of **ALL** income tax withheld. If both a and b apply, enter the year effective and "EXEMPT" here ▶   Year

  c If you entered "EXEMPT" on line 6b, are you a full-time student? . . . . ☐Yes ☐No

Under penalties of perjury, I certify that I am entitled to the number of withholding allowances claimed on this certificate, or if claiming exemption from withholding, that I am entitled to claim the exempt status

Employee's signature ▶   Date ▶   , 19

7 Employer's name and address (**Employer: Complete 7, 8, and 9 only if sending to IRS**)	8 Office code	9 Employer identification number

- Detach along this line. Give the top part of this form to employer, keep the lower part for your records - - - - - - - - - - - - - - - - -

Privacy Act and Paperwork Reduction Act Notice.—If you do not give your employer a certificate, you will be treated as a single person with no withholding allowances as required by law. We ask for this information to carry out the Internal Revenue laws of the United States. We may give the information to the Dept. of Justice for civil or criminal litigation and to the States and the District of Columbia for use in administering their tax laws.

Purpose.—The law requires that you complete Form W-4 so that your employer can withhold Federal income tax from your pay. Your Form W-4 remains in effect until you change it or, if you entered "EXEMPT" on line 6b above, until February 15 of next year. By correctly completing this form, you can fit the amount of tax withheld from your wages to your tax liability.

If you got a large refund last year, you may be having too much tax withheld. If so, you may want to increase the number of your allowances on line 4 by claiming any other allowances you are entitled to. The kinds of allowances, and how to figure them, are explained in detail below.

If you owed a large amount of tax last year, you may not be having enough tax withheld. If so, you can claim fewer allowances on line 4, or ask that an additional amount be withheld on line 5, or both.

If the number of withholding allowances you are entitled to claim decreases to less than you are now claiming, you must file a new W-4 with your employer within 10 days.

The instructions below explain how to fill in Form W-4. **Publication 505**, Tax Withholding and Estimated Tax, contains more information on withholding. You can get it from most IRS offices.

For more information about who qualifies as your dependent, what deductions you can take, and what tax credits you qualify for, see the Form 1040 Instructions.

You may be fined $500 if you file, with no reasonable basis, a W-4 that results in less tax being withheld than is properly allowable. In addition, criminal penalties apply for willfully supplying false or fraudulent information or failing to supply information requiring an increase in withholding.

Line-By-Line Instructions

Fill in the identifying information in Boxes 1 and 2. If you are married and want tax withheld at the regular rate for married persons, check "Married" in Box 3. If you are married and want tax withheld at the higher Single rate (because both you and your spouse work, for example), check "Married, but withhold at higher Single rate" in Box 3.

Line 4 of Form W-4

Total number of allowances.—Use the worksheet on page 2 to figure your allowances. Add the number of allowances for each category explained below. Enter the total on line 4.

If you are single and hold more than one job, you may not claim the same allowances with more than one employer at the same time. If you are married and both you and your spouse are employed, you may not both claim the same allowances with both of your employers at the same time. To have the highest amount of tax withheld, claim "0" allowances on line 4.

A. Personal allowances.—You can claim the following personal allowances:

1 for yourself, 1 if you are 65 or older, and 1 if you are blind.

If you are married and your spouse either does not work or is not claiming his or her allowances on a separate W-4, you may also claim the following allowances: 1 for your spouse, 1 if your spouse is 65 or older, and 1 if your spouse is blind.

B. Special withholding allowance.—Claim the special withholding allowance if you are single and have one job or you are married, have one job, and your spouse does not work. You may still claim this allowance so long as the total wages earned on other jobs by you or your spouse (or both) is 10% or less of the combined total wages. Use this special withholding allowance only to figure your withholding. Do not claim it when you file your return.

C. Allowances for dependents.—You may claim one allowance for each dependent you will be able to claim on your Federal income tax return.

Note: If you are not claiming any deductions or credits, skip D and E, add lines A, B, and C, enter the total on line F and carry the total over to line 4 of W-4.

Before you claim allowances under D and E, total your non-wage taxable income (interest, dividends, self-employment income, etc.) and subtract this amount from estimated deductions you would otherwise enter in D1. If your non-wage income is greater than the amount of estimated deductions, you cannot claim any allowances under D. Moreover, you should take one-third of the excess (non-wage income over estimated deductions) and add this to the appropriate "A" value in Table 1 if determining allowances under E.

D. Allowances for estimated deductions.—If you expect to itemize deductions, you can claim additional withholding allowances. See Schedule A (Form 1040) for deductions you can itemize.

You can also count deductible amounts you pay for (1) alimony (2) qualified retirement contributions including IRA and Keogh (H.R. 10) plans (3) moving expenses (4) employee business expenses (Part I of Form 2106) (5) the deduction for a married couple when both work (6) net losses shown on Schedules C, D, E, and F (Form 1040), the last line of Part II of Form 4797, and the net operating loss carryover (7) penalty on early withdrawal of savings and (8) charitable contributions for nonitemizers. **Note:** Check with your employer to see if any tax is being withheld on moving expenses or IRA contributions. Do not include these amounts if tax is not being withheld; otherwise, you may be underwithheld. For details, see **Publication 505.**

The deduction allowed a married couple when both work is 10% of the lesser of $30,000 or the qualified earned income of the spouse with the lower income.

Once you have determined these deductions, enter the total on line D1 of the worksheet on page 2 and figure the number of withholding allowances for them.

E. Allowances for tax credits.—If you expect to take credits like those shown on lines 41 through 48 on the 1983 Form 1040 (child care, residential energy, etc.), use the table on top of page 2 to figure the number of additional allowances you can claim. You may estimate these credits. Include the earned income credit if you are not receiving advance payment of it, and any excess social security tax withheld. Also, if you expect to income average, include the amount of the reduction in tax because of averaging when using the table.

Line 5 of Form W-4

Additional amount, if any, you want deducted from each pay.—If you are not having enough tax withheld from your pay, you may ask your employer to withhold more by filling in an additional amount on line 5. Often, married couples, both of whom are working, and persons with two or more jobs need to have additional tax withheld. You may also need to have additional tax withheld because you have income other than wages, such as interest and dividends, capital gains, rents, alimony received, taxable social security benefits, etc. Estimate the amount you will be underwithheld and divide that amount by the number of pay periods in the year. Enter the additional amount you want withheld each pay period on line 5.

Line 6 of Form W-4

Exemption from withholding.—You can claim exemption from withholding only if last year you did not owe any Federal income tax and had a right to a refund of all income tax withheld, **and** this year you do not expect to owe any Federal income tax and expect to have a right to a refund of all income tax withheld. If you qualify, check Boxes 6a and b, write the year exempt status is effective and "EXEMPT" on line 6b, and answer Yes or No to the question on line 6c.

If you want to claim exemption from with-holding next year, you must file a new W-4 with your employer on or before February 15 of next year. If you are not having Federal income tax withheld this year, but expect to have a tax liability next year, the law requires you to give your employer a new W-4 by December 1 of this year. If you are covered by social security, your employer must withhold social security tax.

Your employer must send to IRS any W-4 claiming more than 14 withholding allowances or claiming exemption from withholding if the wages are expected to usually exceed $200 a week. The employer is to complete Boxes 7, 8, and 9 only on copies of the W-4 sent to IRS.

Table 1—For Figuring Your Withholding Allowances For Estimated Tax Credits and Income Averaging (Line E)

Estimated Salaries and Wages from All sources	Single Employees		Head of Household Employees		Married Employees (When Spouse not Employed)		Married Employees (When Both Spouses are Employed)	
	(A)	(B)	(A)	(B)	(A)	(B)	(A)	(B)
Under $15,000	$ 90	$150	$ 30	$150	$ 50	$120	$ 0	$120
15,000-25,000	120	250	0	250	70	170	310	170
25,001-35,000	190	300	0	300	130	250	800	220
35,001-45,000	250	370	0	370	170	320	1,500	250
45,001-55,000	690	370	0	370	230	340	2,210	330
55,001-65,000	1,470	370	220	370	310	370	3,020	330
Over 65,000	2,460	370	920	370	680	370	3,400	370

Worksheet to Figure Your Withholding Allowances to be Entered on Line 4 of Form W-4

A Personal allowances ▶ **A**

B Special withholding allowance (not to exceed 1 allowance—see instructions on page 1) ▶ **B**

C Allowances for dependents ▶ **C**

If you are not claiming any deductions or credits, skip lines D and E.

D Allowances for estimated deductions:

   1 Enter the total amount of your estimated itemized deductions, alimony payments, qualified retirement contributions including IRA and Keogh (H.R. 10) plans, deduction for a married couple when both work, business losses including net operating loss carryovers, moving expenses, employee business expenses, penalty on early withdrawal of savings, and charitable contributions for nonitemizers for the year. ▶ **1** $

   2 If you do not plan to itemize deductions, enter $500 on line D2. If you plan to itemize, find your total estimated salaries and wages amount in the left column of the table below. (Include salaries and wages of both spouses.) Read across to the right and find the amount from the column that applies to you. Enter that amount on line D2 ▶ **2** $

Estimated salaries and wages from all sources:	Single and Head of Household Employees (only one job)	Married Employees (one spouse working and one job only)	Employees with more than one job or Married Employees with both spouses working
Under $15,000	$2,800	$3,900	40%
15,000-35,000	2,800	3,900	23% of estimated salaries and wages
35,001-50,000	8% of estimated salaries and wages	3,900	20%
Over $50,000	10% of estimated salaries and wages	7% of estimated salaries and wages	18%

   3 Subtract line D2 from line D1 (But not less than zero) ▶ **3** $

   4 Divide the amount on line D3 by $1,000 (increase any fraction to the next whole number). Enter here ▶ **D**

E Allowances for tax credits and income averaging: use Table 1 above for figuring withholding allowances

   1 Enter tax credits, excess social security tax withheld, and tax reduction from income averaging $

   2 Enter the column (A) amount from Table 1 for your salary range and filing status (single, etc.). However, enter 0 if you claim 1 or more allowances on line D4 $

   3 Subtract line 2 from line 1 (If zero or less, do not complete lines 4 and 5) $

   4 Find the column (B) amount from Table 1 for your salary range and filing status $

   5 Divide line 3 by line 4. Increase any fraction to the next whole number. This is the maximum number of withholding allowances for tax credits and income averaging. Enter here ▶ **E**

   Example: A taxpayer who expects to file a Federal income tax return as a single person estimates annual wages of $12,000 and tax credits of $650. The $12,000 falls in the wage bracket of under $15,000. The value in column (A) is 90. Subtracting this from the estimated credits of 650 leaves 560. The value in column (B) is 150. Dividing 560 by 150 gives 3.7. Since any fraction is increased to the next whole number, show 4 on line E.

F Total (add lines A through E). Enter total here and on line 4 of Form W-4 ▶ **F**

¹ If you earn 10% or less of your total wages from other jobs or one spouse earns 10% or less of the couple's combined total wages, you can use the "Single and Head of Household Employees (only one job)" or "Married Employees (one spouse working and one job only)" table, whichever is appropriate.

I have filled out the 1040 Form depicting Hazel Hayworth as a single person deriving her income solely from her business. Since this is her first year, the business was light, and gave her a smaller income that she will have in the future. If she had been a married person, then her spouse's income would also be included on the form with deductions taken for his work needs that are deductible.

The income statement figures have been transferred to the Profit (or Loss) From Business or Profession form schedule C to show the Internal Revenue service how the net income figure was arrived at. An example of the "Cost of Sales" calculation is on the back of the form as well as the depreciation schedule. The depreciation method used was the straight-line method, which is used by most small businesses. Since Hazel's automobile is not used solely for business, I did not include it on the schedule. We will talk about that later.

If Hazel had itemized her deductions, such figures would have apeared on schedules A & B—Itemized Deductions AND Interest Income. Unless the taxpayer has a large number of deductions, such as property taxes, along with medical, losses, thefts, etc., it is usless to itemize. Most of Hazel's legal deductions are taken in her business income statement and we will go into that now.

Following are some of the deductions most commonly misunderstood. If taken, they might possibly be disallowed by the IRS.

Items to Be Sure of Before You Deduct Them

*Automobile Expense.

The entire cost of operating an automobile cannot be charged to the business unless it is used *exclusively* for the business. To be used exclusively it must be garaged at the business or in the vicinity of the business; and not used to drive back and forth from home. Yes, I know. It is being done every day. Many insurance companies will refuse coverage of an automobile unless it is properly garaged because of the possibility of theft and vandalism. There are actual instances when the closest available garage was across the street from the owner, and was allowed as a business expenditure. It would be best to take this up with your tax advisor.

Gasoline, oil, and tire expenses cannot be deducted in total for the operation of an automobile unless it is used totally for the business. If used partly for family transportation or recreation, then only that portion or percentage of the cost which was incurred in business use will be allowed.

You can take depreciation deductions for the car, but only if it is used at least 50% of the time for business. Only that portion of the year's depreciation that is used for business is deductible. When the car is used 80 percent of the time for business, you can deduct only 80 percent of the depreciation allowance.

If you use your car to drive to Los Angeles to view a fashion show (assuming your store is a clothing store) or to purchase merchandise for sale in your store, that trip is deductible. If you use it to go to Los Angeles (or New York, or wherever) to see a movie or a football game, it is not deductible. An automobile which is not used exclusively for business can be prorated to the business by the mileage you figure was used in carrying on your business.

Business automobile expenses are taken on Schedule C for proprietors.

*Entertainment Expense.

It has often been said that there is more business done on a golf course by real estate salespeople or insurance agents than in the office. In that situation, golf being an entertainment, it is deductible as a legitimate expense. However, if a grocery store owner takes his best friend out on the course for a weekend, he cannot share the same privilege, and would find his golf fees disallowed.

Taking a business person to lunch, or purchasing football tickets for a very good client, are both tax deductible, if the situation is right. But the taxpayer must prove that the entertainment involved was strictly to carry on a part of business which couldn't have been transacted elsewhere, or to create an "atmosphere" which would help a certain type of sale be made.

A small business owner could have entertainment expense that could be legal. Assuming you have an important salesperson coming whose sales to you could be very beneficial, taking the salesperson to a quiet restaurant or bar is often the easiest way of finding privacy while talking business. In that instance, that bit of entertainment expense would be legal.

For an entertainment expense to be deductible, business must actually be discussed either during or immediately before or after the entertainment. "Immediately" has a rather broad meaning. For example, suppose an out of town client comes into town on Wednesday evening. You take him or her out to dinner. You do not discuss business, but on Thursday you conduct a lengthy business meeting. This counts as a business discussion immediately after the entertainment. An important point is that under the tax law only 80% of your business entertainment expenses are deductible. Record 100% of the expense in your ledger. Then bring the entire amount on to Schedule C of your tax return for the year. The return will require you to show the 100% figure and the deductible amount.

Entertaining your local salesperson at a bar on Friday night just for the fun of it is not tax deductible. In deducting the entertainment as a business expense, make certain that you can prove it was business incurred. Then it could be posted to your check register and end up in Operating Expenses.

*Travel Expense.

This type of expense is very similar to auto expense except it can be done by bus, train, or by flying, as well as driving your own car. It is another expense which the taxpayer must prove was incurred in the line of business. To be deductible, the cost of travel must have been incurred while performing some business duty.

A farmer who wants to upgrade his livestock might fly to some larger city to attend a stock show in order to buy a breed of pig, a better milk cow, or a better strain of seed. He might also travel to conventions, seminars, or courses where he might learn something new which will help him on his farm. Such travel would be deductible.

The small business person who drives or flies to another city to attend a meeting to learn something new about the business would be doing it in order to upgrade and improve the business. Such travel would be deductible and would include lodging if necessary. If the spouse went along, his or her portion would not be deductible unless the spouse's presence was necessary to the business.

When traveling, you should record your meal expenses and other travel expenses separately. That's because only 80% of your business meals are deductible, even if you eat them alone while traveling on business. Your other business travel expenses are 100% deductible.

*Moving Expenses

Anyone who has to move six rooms of furniture, two kids, a dog, and an anxious spouse should be able to deduct all expenses twice over and get another deduction for the trauma caused by the tension involved in leaving a home you have lived in for so long.

But it isn't so.

In order to take a deduction for moving, it is necessary to prove that such a move was necessary to keep your job, or operate your business. Moving into a better neighborhood, or to be closer to the job, doesn't count. It must be necessary to move in order to *have the job* or business, and prove that not moving would restrain you from performing the duties of your job. However, moving a business from one place to another *is* deductible.

This deduction would be taken on schedule A & B.

*Education.

People often go to night school to learn more about their field. Such learning fees would be deductible as an educational expense. Going to school to learn how to program a computer while you are working as a warehouseman would not be deductible. The cost of education must be in the form of improvement in your present occupation or business, to make you more valuable to the company, and to help you to get ahead in your present profession or vocation.

Taking a course in Business Administration while operating your small business would, in my opinion, be a deductible expense. But check with your own tax advisor. This book was written to alert you to the pitfalls of taxes, not extend the perfect answers to every situation. Also remember that even some of the IRS auditors are not clear on all deductible expenses, and they are sometimes open to argument. What might be deductible one year may not be the next. So do remember to confer with a tax advisor whenever there is a question.

Self-Employment Tax Installments

Earlier we went over how you should compute the income and FICA tax withholding and payments for your employees. If your business is incorporated, you will be treated as an employee and must compute the income and FICA tax for yourself just the same as you do for other employees. At this point, you probably are a proprietor and do not receive a regular salary, so you do not have wage withholding. But you still must "pay-as-you-go" for both income taxes and social security taxes. You must prepay your federal income tax and social security tax in quarterly installments on April 15, July 15, October 15, and January 15. The payments are made with Form 1040ES, which is available from any IRS office. Once you have filed a 1040ES for a quarter, the IRS will send you a year's worth of computer preprinted forms so all you have to do for future installments is fill in the amount and enclose a check.

Each payment with Form 1040ES is the payment of two taxes: the federal income tax and the self-employment tax. (A state income tax will have a similar form and quarterly payment requirement.)

Your federal income tax must be paid in installments. You must prepay at least 90% of this year's tax liability or 100% of last year's tax bill, whichever you choose. The prepayments must be made in equal quarterly installments. This means you must estimate your taxable income for the year, figure the tax on that estimate, divide by four, and pay the result with Form 1040ES each quarter. Or you can divide last year's tax bill by four and pay that amount with Form 1040ES. If you do not prepay your taxes, you will have to pay a penalty when you eventually file your return and pay the taxes. The penalty is interest at the rate of one percent above the federal short-term interest rate and is adjusted quarterly.

The self-employment tax is the self-employed person's version of the social security tax. It is imposed on your net income from self-employment. That is your gross income minus the allowed business deductions. You might recall that the combined employer and employee tax rate for the FICA tax is 15.02% (7.51% each for the employer and employee). The self-employment tax rate is the same as the combined employer-employee rate. That means the self-employment tax is 15.02% in 1988 and 1989 and 15.30% in 1990. This tax comes right out of your net income, so you want to be careful to budget for it. Many new business owners are not aware of the self-employment tax and get into financial trouble by neglecting to budget for it. Your self-employment tax is estimated the same as your estimated income tax payments. You must estimate what the tax bill will be at the end of the year, divide by four, and pay the resulting amount each quarter.

When you are self-employed, you must file Schedule SE with your tax return. If you failed to prepay your taxes, you also must file Form 2210. On this form you will compute the penalty for failure to prepay. It might be possible to avoid the penalty when your income unexpectedly increased during the year. If that happened to you, complete Part III of Form 2210. It is fairly complicated, but it might save you a substantial amount of money.

---

*Form 1099

Some Other Forms for You to Think About

The tax law requires you to report to the IRS many payments you make to others during the year. Anyone who is engaged in a trade or business must report to the IRS anytime payments totaling more than $600 during the year are made to anyone other than a corporation or employee. A copy of the statement also must be furnished to the payee. The payments are reported on Form 1099. Form 1099 has grown to a whole series of forms. I will list the numbers and what they are so that you will be able to determine which should be filed.

You must also file a report with the IRS whenever you receive more than $10,000 in cash from anyone during the year. When money is received in a series of transactions, you must add these together to determine if the $10,000 level is reached. The report must be filed on Form 8300. For purposes of this rule, bank checks, traveler's checks, and similar negotiable instruments are not treated as cash. If you regularly receive large amounts of money from individual customers or clients you should get Form 8300 and the instructions to determine your reporting responsibility. If you have any questions, it is a good idea to consult an attorney with these questions.

1099 DIV . . . . Statement for Recipients of Dividends and Distributions.

1099 INT . . . . Statement for Recipients of Interest Income.

1099 L . . . . U.S. Information Return Distributions/Liquidations During Calendar Year.

1099 MED . . . . U.S. Information Return for Recipients of Medical and Health Care Payments.

1099 MISC . . . . U.S. Information Return for Recipients of Miscellaneous Income.

1099 OID . . . . U.S. Information Return for Original Issue of Discount.

1099 PATR . . . . Statement for Recipients (Patrons) of Taxable Distributions Received from Cooperatives.

1099 R . . . . Statements for Recipients of Lump-Sum Distributions from Profit-Sharing and Retirement Plans.

*Employee's Withholding Certificate Form W-4.

This is one form that I feel certain everyone is familiar with, even if they are just now going into business for themselves and do not have employees. Everyone has worked at sometime for someone else and had to fill out a W-4 form to inform the employer how to make deductions to take on the withholding of income taxes from the paycheck. Following is a copy of the form. Be sure any employees in your business complete this form upon hiring.

Form **W-4**
(Rev. January 1982)

Department of the Treasury—Internal Revenue Service

Employee's Withholding Allowance Certificate

OMB No. 1545-0010
Expires 4-30-83

1 Type or print your full name

MARY LOUISE WILSON

Home address (number and street or rural route)

1812 FRONT STREET

City or town, State, and ZIP code

SANTA CRUZ, CALIFORNIA 95060

2 Your social security number

541 - 42 - 7361

3 Marital Status

☐ Single ☒ Married
☐ Married, but withhold at higher Single rate

Note: If married, but legally separated, or spouse is a nonresident alien, check the Single box.

4 Total number of allowances you are claiming (from line F of the worksheet on page 2) **2**

5 Additional amount, if any, you want deducted from each pay . . . . $

6 I claim exemption from withholding because (see instructions and check boxes below that apply):

  a ☐ Last year I did not owe any Federal income tax and had a right to a full refund of **ALL** income tax withheld, **AND**

  b ☐ This year I do not expect to owe any Federal income tax and expect to have a right to a full refund of **ALL** income tax withheld. If both a and b apply, enter "EXEMPT" here . . . . ▶

  c If you entered "EXEMPT" on line 6b, are you a full-time student? . . . . ☐ Yes ☐ No

Under the penalties of perjury, I certify that I am entitled to the number of withholding allowances claimed on this certificate, or if claiming exemption from withholding, that I am entitled to claim the exempt status.

Employee's signature ▶ *Mary Louise Wilson* Date ▶ OCT. 16 , 19

7 Employer's name and address (including ZIP code) (FOR EMPLOYER'S USE ONLY)

HAZEL'S BOUTIQUE, 921 HAYWOOD DR.
SANTA CRUZ, CALIFORNIA 95062

8 Office code

9 Employer identification number

94-1669471

You get to depreciate your business assets. This means that you can deduct part of the cost over a period of years. The period depends on the type of asset you have. But there is a better way of treating the purchase of new business assets that many small business owners overlook. You can deduct as a business expense the cost of some assets in the year they are acquired. You can deduct up to $10,000 of the cost of new equipment each year. You can deduct all of the cost of a particular piece of property or a portion of the cost of several assets. Just be sure to designate your choice on Form 4562 when you file the tax return.

When you take the election, you can still depreciate the property if you do not expense the entire cost. You subtract the amount that was expensed from the cost, and depreciate the remainder of the cost. Read the instructions with Form 4562 carefully.

The annual expense amount is reduced as your business grows. When the cost of new property for the year exceeds $200,000, the expense amount is reduced by the excess. For example, if you acquire $205,000 of property during the year, you can expense no more than $5,000 during the year. The amount you expense during the year also cannot exceed the amount of your taxable income for the year from the business. That means that the expensing election cannot be used to generate a tax loss.

Your home office deduction cannot exceed your net income from the business. For example, suppose you earned a gross income of $25,000 from your home business and had business expenses of $20,000, not including the home office expenses. Your home office expenses for the year come to $6,000. You can deduct only $5,000 of the office expenses.

The other $1,000 are simply suspended. You can deduct them in a future year when your net income exceeds the home office expenses for that year.

An office in the home—how can we deduct the cost of it? An office in the home is deductible, but . . . You must be able to prove that one or more rooms of the house is/are used *exclusively* for transacting business or doing something to help carry on the business. It must have a desk or table, perhaps a typewriter or a telephone extension and other equipment that shows you actually carry on part of your business activities from that room. This could involve billing customers each month, calling salespeople in regards to purchases, doing bookkeeping or some other activity that pertains to the business.

You can take a deduction which is part of your total rent or mortgage payment, depending on how much of the house is being used. You can calculate this by taking the number of rooms and dividing it into the monthly rent/mortgage figure. If you have three bedrooms, living room, dining room, and kitchen; you have six rooms. In figuring a deduction, let's assume your monthly rent or mortgage payment is $360. You take one-sixth (because you have six rooms) of $360, or $60.00 as a deduction for the room you use for business purposes. You could also deduct one-sixth of the utilities. The telephone charge would be any amount over the basic charge which was incurred in business. Such charges might be extension phone charges, long distance calls, or a percentage of local calls.

Clothing as a deduction—when can you deduct it? Many professional people do deduct the cost of clothing as an expense and the IRS does not question it. These people are performers who must wear stage costumes, or doctors, dentists, dental hygienists, nurses, waitresses, and waiters. You can deduct some costs of clothing also if you can show that it is for items that you would not *normally wear* on the street or for daily use.

Self-employed individuals now are able to deduct a portion of their health insurance premiums. In the past, these expenses were considered nondeductible personal expenses. But now you are allowed to deduct 25% of health insurance premiums paid to insure you, your spouse, and your dependents. This covers only health insurance. Other medical expenses are deductible the same as for other taxpayers on Schedule A. Any health insurance premiums paid for your employees are fully deductible as business expenses.

The end of the year offers some unique opportunities to reduce your tax bill, though these opportunities are not as numerous as they were a few years ago. Throughout this book we've assumed that you have a cash basis accounting method. This means that in most cases an amount is not included in your income until you actually receive it. And expenses are deductible when you mail the check or put the expense on the credit card. If you near the end of the year and want to reduce your taxes a bit, you can take several steps. You can purchase office supplies and other deductible items, making sure that you mail a check in payment or put the item on your credit card by December 31. That way you are sure the items will be deductible this year instead of having to wait a year. Likewise, you can delay sending out bills for a few weeks in December. That way you won't receive payments until after December

31. By doing this you will delay your receiving the money by only a matter of weeks, but the income will be on next year's tax return instead of this year's.

If Hazel Hayworth wears maroon-and-tan colored jackets in the store in order to keep her regular clothing clean and free from wear-and-tear, those jackets are deductible.

If Arnold Sims wears tan shirts in his television shop which have a legend on the back reading "Sim's T.V. Repair" or "Sim's T.V. Sales," such shirts would be deductible. If his workers also wear smocks to keep their street clothes clean, such costs would be deductible.

White jacket worn by doctors, white dresses worn by nurses, safety shoes, safety glasses—all of these are deductible. Ordinary clothing, shoes, and glasses are not.

Non-deductible Expenses

Some of the many non-deductible expenses include:

Traffic fines.

Bus fare to work.

Legal fees incurred in the preparation of a will.

Labor from the store to fix your house or yard.

Extensive building improvements (additions to a rented building would be lease-hold improvements and must be amortized over a period of years).

Improvements to your building (such improvements are classified as leasehold improvements and are added to the Capital Assets in the asset section and amortized over a period of years).

Cost of acquiring, defending, or clearing the title to property.

Political or campaign expenses or contributions.

Life insurance (unless it is a fringe benefit for the employee and you are not the beneficiary).

One Final Word

Up to this point, I have attempted to show the new business owner what is necessary to set up a simple bookkeeping system and to alert him/her to the pitfalls of being "self-employed." Being in a business for oneself is a marvelous feeling of independence. However, I want to impress on you at this time that my book is to show you "how to do it yourself" up to a point. That is, keeping the records and preparing an Income Statement for your tax person or firm. After that, it is a good idea to have a competent tax advisor do the final work of preparing the returns for you. This way may be a bit more expensive, but it is well worth it in the satisfaction of knowing everything has been done properly, and on time.

The bookkeeper for a small business should have no problems in taking care of the State and Federal Quarterly withholding and sales taxes. To help the new bookkeeper/accountant, the following is a calendar of taxes, which are due, and when to file them.

Tax Calendar and Checklist

Following are excerpts from the IRS publication 509 "Tax Calendar and Check List" for a recent year. The complete publication can be obtained from your nearest IRS office.

January

During the month, you may deposit the appropriate amounts of the following taxes: Income taxes and FICA taxes withheld, plus the employer's portion of the Social Security taxes. These are sent to a Federal bank (probably your own). Use Form 501. Excise taxes, Form 504. Federal unemployment tax, Form 508.

Employers should give the employee Copy B and C of Form W-2, which states what the gross earnings were and what the amount of withholdings were, as soon as possible in this month.

January 15.

Individuals must pay the balance due on the previous year's estimated income tax.

A farmer or fisherman is excused from filing a declaration of estimated tax if he files his return and pays the full amount of his tax on or before March 1st following the close of his taxable (calendar) year.

January 31.

File Form 941 for income tax withheld and Social Security taxes for the fourth quarter of the previous year, and pay any taxes due. If the quarterly tax liability as shown on Form 941 (reduced by any deposits during the quarter) is $500 or more, the unpaid balance must be deposited with a depository. Use Form 501. *

You are now filing the tax Form 941 for the last quarter of the year and must enclose copies of the W-2 forms of employees as well as a recap of all the 941's for the year. Be certain the totals of the W-2's gross equal your bookkeeping gross wages, and the totals of the gross wages of the four quarterly returns. Also, the Income Tax withheld and the FICA taxes withheld must jibe with your bookkeeping records. If you have been careful with your calculations during the year, this will be a simple matter.

February 15

Social Security and Federal Income taxes (of $500. or more) withheld in January should be deposited with your depository bank. Use Form 501.

March 15.

Social Security and Federal Income taxes (of $500. or more) withheld in February should be deposited. Use Form 501.

Corporations must file an income tax return, Form 1120, or apply for an extension, Form 7004, and pay to a depository at least 50% of the balance of tax still due. Use Form 503.

*Federal deposits could be more frequently required than illustrated here. Check with your IRS office.

April 15.

Individuals must file a declaration of estimated income tax (including self-employment tax) for the current year and pay at least 25% of such tax. Use Form 1040ES.

Partnerships must file a return of income for the previous years. Use Form 1065.

April 30.

File Form 941 quarterly tax return for withholding Social Security and Federal Income taxes. Pay balance due if not already deposited.

May 15.

Deposit Social and Federal Income taxes (of $500. or more) withheld in April.

June 15.

Individuals must pay the second installment of estimated income tax for the current year. Use Form 1040ES.

Corporations must pay the balance of previous year income tax liability. The second installment of 25% of current estimated tax liability is due. Payments are made to depository using Form 503.

Deposit Social Security and Federal Income taxes (of $500. or more) withheld in May to the depository bank.

July 31.

File Form 941 quarterly tax return for withholding Social Security and Federal Income taxes. Pay balance due if not already deposited.

August 15.

Deposit Social Security and Federal Income taxes (of $500. or more) withheld in July from employees.

September 15.

Individuals must pay the third installment of estimated income tax for the current year. Use Form 1040ES

Corporations must pay to a depository the third installment of 25% of the current year estimated income tax. Use Form 503.

Deposit Federal Income and Social Security taxes (of $500. or more) withheld in August.

October 31.

File Form 941 for Income and Social Security taxes withheld for the third quarter of the year. Pay any balance due.

November 15.

Deposit withholding taxes (of $500. or more) withheld in October.

December 15.

Corporations must pay to a depository the fourth installment of 25% of the current year estimated income tax. Use Form 503.

Deposit Income and Social Security taxes withheld in November. (The Social Security taxes for December will be deposited in January of the following year and included on the final return Form 941, which will be due January 31st of the following year.)

For additional information on tax due dates, contact your local IRS office or consult your tax advisor.

9

Accounting for the Expanding Business

Using our flatform ledger is a good way of keeping records for tax purposes for the very small business. But it does have one major drawback. If the business expands rapidly, it soon outgrows the usefulness of the flatform. It is limited to the number of accounts which can be added to it without having to make new sheets each time. If new sheets had to be made each quarter in order to add new accounts that come into being, the work would soon become an endless chore.

There is an easier way.

Now that you have learned what accounting is all about, and know how the accounts should be arranged in a ledger, it is a simple matter to transfer our totals from the last "Total to Date" into a regular ledger. We can carry on from there.

In the regular General Ledger, each account usually occupies a separate sheet, or page, by itself. In the small business, we can place a number of accounts on one sheet which has multiple columns in the manner of our columnar pad. This occurs mostly in the expense items of the operating expense section. Suppose we make such a transition from our flatform ledger sheets into a regular book binder and find out what kind of set-up we need.

During my years of public accounting, most of it in the small business field (bar, shoe shop, small grocery store, small garage, small apparel store, toy shop, etc.), I have found the 11" x 11" size binder to be most suitable for the work to be done. It is small enough to be easily handled yet still large enough to do the job at hand. These ledgers can be purchased at any office supply store.

The cost of a good binder is nominal, running around $15.00 for the empty binder and $.13 per sheet for the forms. You should purchase at least a dozen sheets of each of the daily journals, and possibly twenty or thirty of the single-page ledger sheets (Burroughs Form C16). These are used for the Assets, the Liabilities, Sales, and Cost of Sales. The operating expenses are posted on form Burroughs C46. If your store doesn't have these, ask for an equivalent of the numbers given. In putting together your first ledger, I recommend certain sheets because you will find them very similar to the makeshift sheets we have been using in the instructions. This was done purposely so that the book-keeper would feel no disorientation in making the transfer to the regular general ledger.

Here are the sheets I have found most suitable for the 11" x 11" ledger.

First the ledger. Wilmer Service Line puts out a sturdy ledger for approximately $15.00, but there are others. Be sure to ask for the 11" x 11" binder.

Cash Received Sheets—	11" x 11" —Burroughs C71—buy 12
Check Distribution—	11" x 11" —Burroughs C80—buy 12
Journal Entries—	11" x 11" —Burroughs C10—buy 6
Ledger Sheets—	11" x 11" —Burroughs C16—buy 20
Expense Sheets—	11" x 11" —Burroughs C46—buy 6

Total—56 sheets @ $.13 = $7.28 plus $15.00 = $22.28*

If you prefer, a binder which includes sheets and separaters with tabs marking the separate sections of the ledger, can be purchased for approximately $30.00. This is a reasonable price for good working material for an accounting system.

In setting up your own ledger, if the above sheets are not available, substitutes can be found by the store clerk if you give him the form name and number.

If you can, it is a good point to obtain separation sheets to place between the groups. These will mark the sections of the ledger so that any section can be found easily. Such sheets can be purchased at the supply store either already-titled, or with attachable name tabs.

In putting the ledger together, place the groups of sheets in it in the following sequence so that the sheets most used are at the top and easiest to reach.

What Goes in the Ledger

1. Cash Received or Sales Sheets
2. Check Register or Distribution Sheets
3. Journal Entries Sheets
4. Assets Ledger Sheets
5. Liabilities Ledger Sheets
6. Income Ledger Sheets
7. Cost of Sales Ledger Sheets
8. Operating Expense Ledger Sheets

Put a separator in front of each group of sheets with the name tab which applies. Now you have your ledger.

*Prices subject to change.

Activating the Ledger

To activate the ledger, post the figures from the last total or year-to-date column onto the top of the appropriate account sheet *above the red line* in the "balance" column. In the description space, enter the notation "Opening entries." In the posting reference column write or print "From flatform." If the auditor looks at the entry, you will probably be asked what a "flatform" is, and you can then hand him the little jewel. He can then see that your figures have a positive basis for entry in the new ledger.

We have not included Invoice Register sheets in our ledger because we are still on the cash basis of accounting. We do not need them. Until the business becomes large enough to warrant their use, you will have less work to do without them.

Now that you have the ledger prepared, write in the account names from the flatform sheets. Work through the flatform or your Chart of Accounts. These should have the same account names on them. If you prepared an Income Statement and Balance Sheet on the last month or year to date, you not only have the accounts but also the amounts needed to open your new ledger. I have often set up a new ledger from a computer print-out sheet.

Posting

Start posting your opening entries from the last figure on the flatform, which is the total of the year-to-date. Post the figure above the red line in the "balance" column. This figure should be written in ink, but the balances below the red line are usually entered in pencil. Everything else is entered in ink except the subtotals of the columns of the operating expense sheets. These pencilled totals are the figures for the year-to-date on these sheets. The total of these, taken across the pages, should equal the total that is in the balance column.

When the opening entries are completed, you will be ready for your first monthly posting from your new daily journals. (The new ledger Cash-Received sheets and Check-Distribution sheets.) When posting, remember that the left column (charges) are really debits from the right side of the check register and the left side of the sales register. In the ledger, the debits are always posted in the left column (charges) and the credits in the right column (credits).

On the new Operating Expense sheets, the individual accounts are posted to a single column. A running total of the column is posted in pencil beneath the month's entry. Remember that you could have figures from two different sources and might have to cram the figures into the space provided. The pencil totals of the figures need to be taken only when a statement is desired. If you do this each month, however, there is less possibility of error.

There is very little else I can say that will give you any comfort in posting your first figures in the new general ledger. If you are in doubt, post them in pencil and go over them with ink when you are certain that everything is in the proper place and balances. With the experience you have obtained from posting the flatform ledger sheets, I'm sure you will find your work clear sailing from here on. If you should hit a snag, or have a problem, ask a question of your friendly Public Accountant. If the work

Figure 28

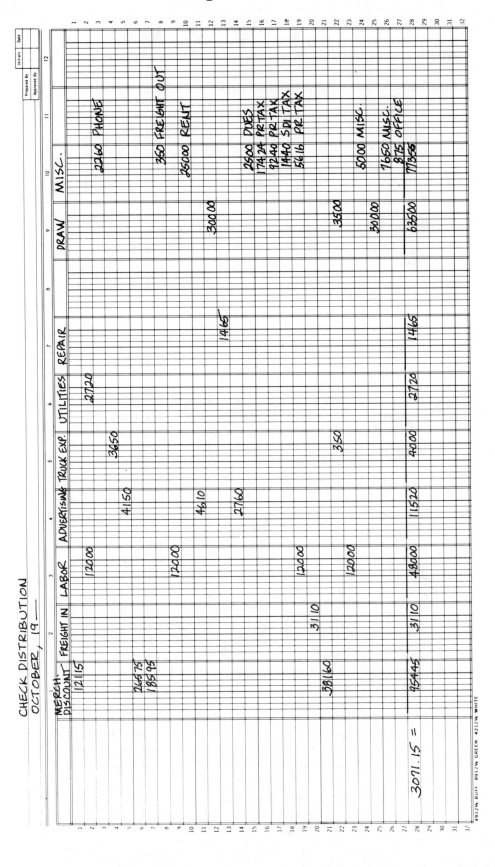

Figure 29

RECORD OF CHECKS DRAWN — OCTOBER, 19___

DRAWN TO:	MISC.	SWH	SDI	FICA	WH	NET CHECK	CK. #	DATE
BANCROFT INDUSTRIES						12115	386	10-7
P.G.E.						2720	387	10-7
JAMES BATES		-0-	120	702	770	10408	388	10-8
PACIFIC TELEPHONE						2260	389	10-8
STANDARD OIL CO.						3650	390	10-8
SENTINEL						4150	391	10-9
WESTERN GIRL						26675	392	10-9
COUNTRY CASUALS (DISCOUNT)	372					18223	393	10-11
UNITED PARCEL						350	394	10-11
JAMES BATES		-0-	120	702	770	10408	395	10-15
WOODWARD & SIMMS						25000	396	10-15
SENTINEL						4610	397	10-15
HOMER WILSON						30000	398	10-16
ED'S GARAGE (DOLLY)						1465	399	10-16
SIEVER'S PAINT SHOP (POSTERS)						2760	400	10-16
BUSINESSMEN'S ASSN.						2600	401	10-18
INTERNAL REVENUE						26664	402	10-18
STATE EMP. DEPT.						7056	403	10-18
JAMES BATES		-0-	120	702	770	10408	404	10-20
R & J TRUCKING						3110	405	10-20
COLO JUMPERS						38160	406	10-21
HOMER WILSON						3500	407	10-28
UNION SERV. STA. (FIX FLAT)						350	408	10-28
JAMES BATES		-0-	120	702	770	10408	409	10-28
J. SLOAN (CLEAN UP)						5000	410	10-29
HOMER WILSON						30000	411	10-29
EVENS CLEANERS						7650	412	10-29
CLOVER MARKET-CASH	DRAW 815					299500 = 3021.15	CASH	10-29
	1247	-0-	480	2808	3080			

49124 BUFF 89124 GREEN 42124 WHITE

Prepared By ____ Approved By ____ Initials ____ Date ____ becomes too much, then it is time to have someone do the wrap-up work. You can still do the individual entries and have the accountant take it from there. The accountant's work will also include Income and financial Statements when needed.

Now that we have reached this point, there is little need for me to rehash material already covered. You don't need it. All I can say is: "You've come a long way . . ." and maybe you should be just a bit proud that you were able to follow through the maze to this point in the book.

Take a moment right now to pat yourself on the back, accept my congratulations and wishes for luck in your accounting. Since you have reached this point, I am confident that you are capable of doing it all yourself.

Figure 30

GENERAL LEDGER — SALES INCOME - LEATHER GOODS

DESCRIPTION	DATE	POSTING REFERENCE	CHARGES	CREDITS	BALANCE
TOTAL TO DATE— SEPTEMBER	19XX	FLAT FORM			995 15

GENERAL LEDGER — SALES INCOME - APPAREL

DESCRIPTION	DATE	POSTING REFERENCE	CHARGES	CREDITS	BALANCE
TOTAL TO DATE— SEPTEMBER	19XX	FLAT FORM			630 57

GENERAL LEDGER — SALES INCOME - SHOES/FOOTWEAR

DESCRIPTION	DATE	POSTING REFERENCE	CHARGES	CREDITS	BALANCE
TOTAL TO DATE— SEPTEMBER	19XX	FLAT FORM			451 93

Figure 31

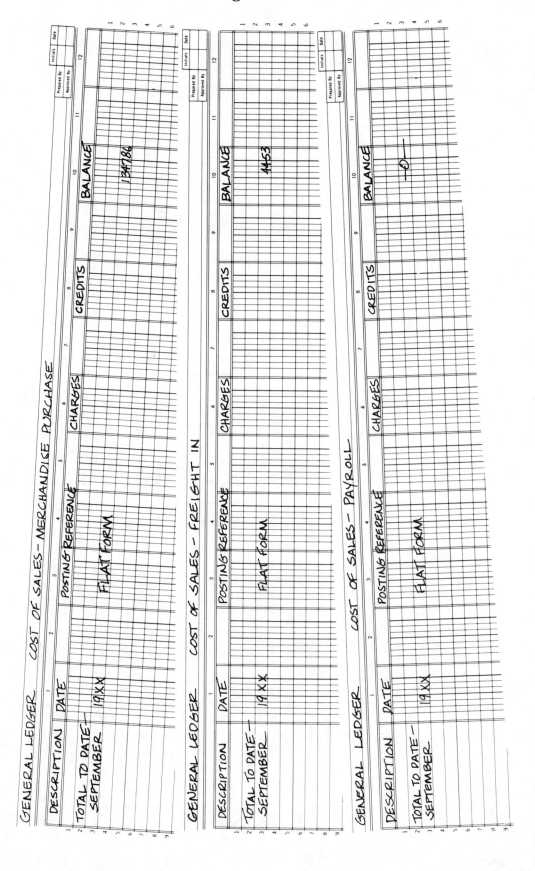

Figure 32

INSURANCE	UTILITIES	TELEPHONE	ADVERTISING	RENT	DATE	DESCRIPTION	POSTING REFERENCE	CHARGES	CREDITS		BALANCE	
1	2	3	4	5	6		7	8	9	10	11	12
252 50	114 50	54 16	171 58	542 00	10/19XX	OPENING ENTRIES					1400 80	
-0-	19 65	27 50	25 00	275 00	/	OCT. EXPENSES	CK#4	422 26			1823 06	
252 50	134 15	81 66	196 58	817 00								

Initials | Date | Prepared By | Approved By

Figure 33

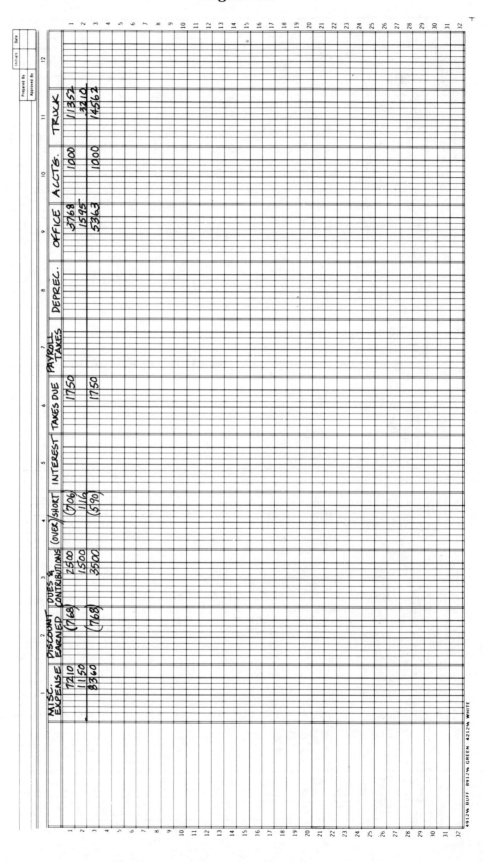

10

A Simple Costing System for the Small Business

We have been using only the retail store in preparing examples of records for the small business. Yet there are other kinds of businesses started by husband-and-wife teams who find they need not only an accurate bookkeeping system but also some means of keeping costs on the work they perform. Among these people can be found the individual house builder, the swimming pool contractor, and the person offering heating and plumbing services.

Accounting for The Contractor

One contractor can often have three or four jobs going at the same time. Often bills for all of these jobs are paid for with one check. Cement purchases from a cement company might be used on three different jobs by the swimming pool contractor. Lumber purchases might go into four different houses at the same time. Because of the various sizes of the jobs it is not possible to divide the total cost by three or four and come up with an accurate cost for each one. It is necessary to have some other method of figuring costs on each job. It is also necessary to keep the materials used on one separate from materials used on the others. This is done by means of job names, numbers, and symbols.

In any business, large or small, whether it be the construction of buildings or the manufacturing of aircraft, the process of cost accounting is the same. It involves the prorating or distribution of materials, labor, and expense costs into the items on which the business wants cost figures. Lockheed might want to prepare costs on an aircraft as a whole, or they might want to break the costs down to the separate components (such as wings, fuselage, motors, etc.). Regardless of the extent to which the breakdown is to be carried, the method is the same. This is dividing the amounts between the various components and accumulating all work that goes into those items by means of symbol to identify the item of work being "costed out."

The example that follows was set up for the Maarten Construction Co. This was an individual who needed a costing system which could be accurate and easily accomplished by a neophyte bookkeeper. In order to post the distribution of the costs at the same time the check was written, I added an extension distribution check sheet to the daily posting distribution sheet. It consisted of the distribution side of the Burroughs C80 form, and was taped so that the cost sheet could be folded back under the check-distribution sheet. By cutting off the peg side at the line number column, it was easy to make the sheet fit and still be able to close the book. In manufacturing, it could be equipment name if a piece of equipment was being costed out.

Maarten Construction
319 Prospect Heights Road
Santa Cruz, CA 95065

Job Cost Items

A. Lumber—Rough Finish
B. Concrete
C. Cabinets—Built-in
D. Glass—Windows and doors
E. Direct Labor
F. Plumbing—Subcontract or parts
G. Built-in appliances
H. Hardware and fixtures
I. Insulation
J. Electrical—Subcontractor or parts
K.
L.
M. Miscellaneous Items—Countertops, Septic tanks, Tile, Mirrors, Fireplaces, Garage Doors
N. Special Equipment Rental
O. Drywall—Sheetrock
P. Floor Covering—Carpet or linoleum
S. Doors
T. Paint costs
U. Roofing
W. Heating and Conditioning
X.
Y. Excavation or grading
Z. Building permits

While posting the amount of the check on the distribution sheet, it is a simple matter to move along the spread-out costing sheet and post in the job column. The amount to be posted depends on the owner (or some employee designated by the owner) to break down the amounts of cost to the jobs. Then the amounts can be written on the check stubs. Unless some responsible person makes the breakdown, the costs will never be accurate, regardless of the quality of the costing system.

If $475.00 worth of lumber is purchased and only a portion of it is used on the Andrews job, then the contractor (or employee) must mark the delivery slip according to the amount delivered to whom. Perhaps only one-third was delivered to Andrews, with a third of the balance being delivered to Harbor High School for the shed they are building. This would leave $211.11 worth of lumber left for a third job.

If properly posted, the delivery slip or the check stub would be posted like this:

Andrews	Rough lumber	$158.33
Harbor High School	Shed floor	105.56
Antinelli	Rough lumber	211.11
TOTAL OF CHECK		$475.00

In posting this check stub, the above figures would be carried over to the Andrews, Harbor High and Antinelli on the cost-distribution sheet and be posted with the accompanying symbol of: A $158.33 HHS A. 105.56, Ant. A 211.11.

The next posting might be for cement purchased and used on two of the jobs. The posting might be Andrews, Concrete 375.65, Antinelli, Concrete 184.95. Total $560.60. In posting to the Check record and cost distribution, the amount written to Los Alamos Concrete would be $560.60 but would be broken down in the Andrews and Antinelli columns, Andrews B $375.65, Antinelli B 184.95.

The same would go for the other types of items being costed out. Direct Labor would be charged to the job using it, being sure to distribute the gross amount. Then at the end of the month, the bookkeeper would have to go through the various columns, add up all the labor and calculate the unemployment insurance paid on the amount of labor used, then do the same with FICA. It is a simple matter because gross wages are used on either item and the percentage charged the employer can be found on the state withholding return. FICA is a known factor, because both the employee and employer pay the same amount, 6.70%.

When the month is completed, the bookkeeper will add up the column of figures to get a total, then recap the various items of work on a scratch sheet in much the way he does the miscellaneous column of the check register. When he has broken down the column to the various job letters, he adds up the figures for the various items of work so that he has a total of each one.

	Andrews		Harbor High		Antinelli
A.	158.33	A.	105.56	A.	211.11
B.	375.65			B.	184.95
C.	131.85			C.	214.21
D.	56.80	D.	43.90		
E.	87.50	E.	94.70	E.	210.20
	810.13		244.16		820.47

When this is accomplished, he posts the breakdown at the bottom of the cost sheet. If not enough space is available at the bottom, post on the back of the cost sheet. When this has been accomplished, post the items to the individual sheets. These are made up from our old standby columnar pad, the Burroughs Form No. H556 Buff. One sheet of the pad can do for a number of months to accumulate the costs as they are needed. It also fits into a looseleaf binder so that it can be kept on the desk, handy for posting when needed.

To start, put the job name or number on the sheet and type in the Item of Work letters in the description space. This sets you up in business, and all you have to do is post each month as you recap it from the cost-distribution sheet. It is simple and effective, and can be changed or enlarged to any degree necessary. Remember that at the end of the month, if there is labor, calculate the employer's FICA by multiplying by the percentage required for FICA, and add this figure to the column. It could be called "Payroll Taxes" so that you will be able to tell at a glance that you have added the taxes into the total. Unemployment insurance is figured the same way, by multiplying the breakdown of labor by the employer rate. At the end of the quarter, you would have to check the amounts to make certain you have added your calculations for the three months, and compare with your total on the tax return. Adjustments will probably have to be made, but that is a small problem. This costing does not have to come down to pennies.

Dividing Overhead Expenses

The overhead expenses have to be divided up at the end of the month. These are worked into each project. I have found this is best accomplished on the "dollar spent" basis. This is done by adding up the total amounts spent on the jobs and prorating the operating costs into them by the percentage of expenses to money spent. This way, the project which cost the most money would carry most of the cost of the overhead.

In order to see how it works, let's dream up some figures and say that our contractor has three jobs going. At the end of the month, he discovers that he has spent on "A" $4,215.19, on "B" $7,211.05, and on "C" $9,811.04. His operating expenses for the month were $2,573.14.

First, add the jobs to get a total of the three amounts. The answer is $21,237.28.

Now, to find out what percentage of the total amount each job would be, do a little calculation. Divide the amount of Job A ($4,215.19) by Total Job ($21,237.28). The answer is .198, or 20%. By doing the same with Job B ($7,211.05), we obtain a percentage figure of .3395, or 34%. The third Job C ($9,811.04) divided by 21,237.38 gives us a percentage figure of .4619, or 46%. If you add the percentage figures (20% + 34% + 46%), you will find that they total 100%. These are the percentage figures we will use to prorate our operating expenses.

Figure 34

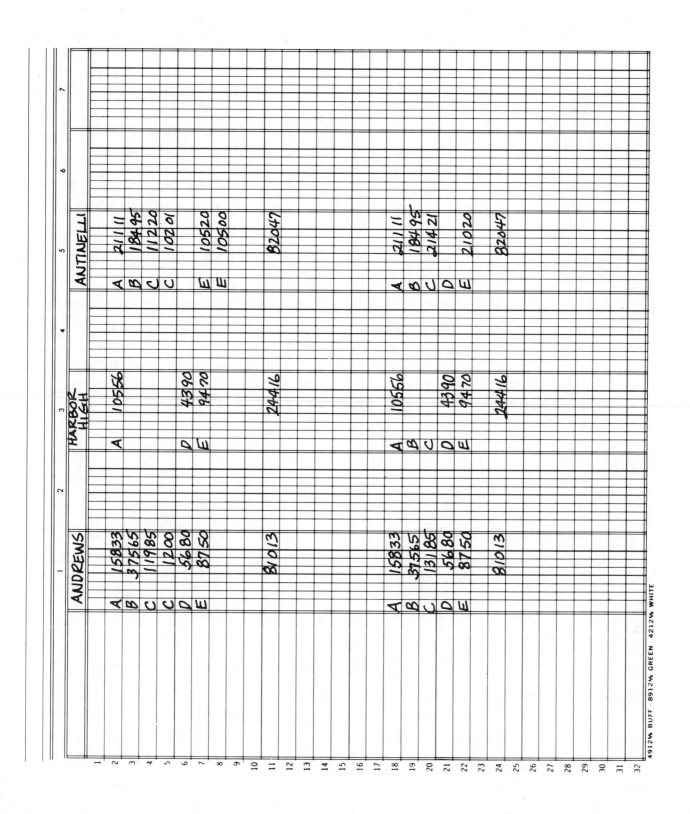

Figure 35

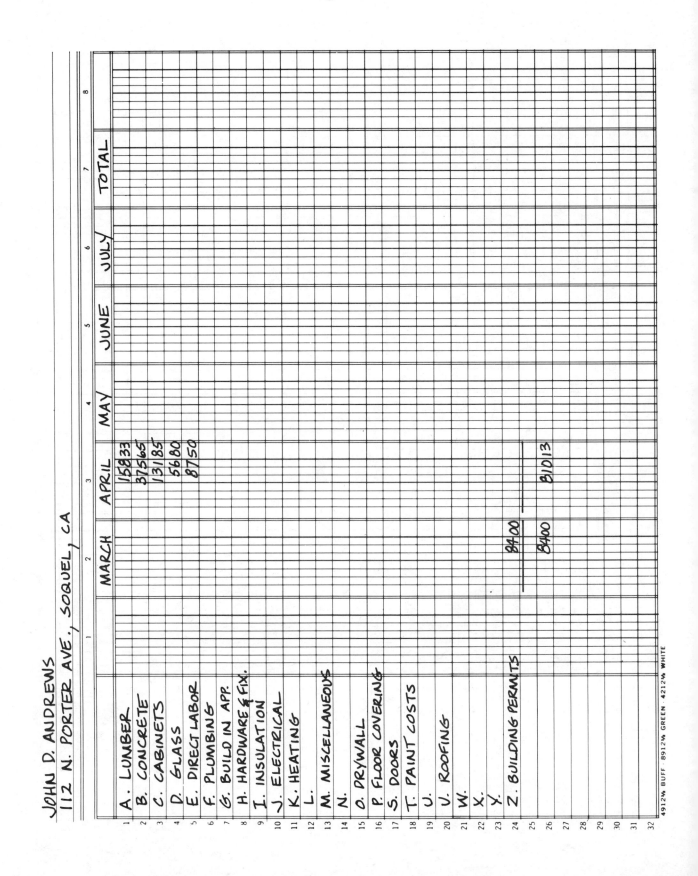

If the first job was 20% of the total money spent, then it should be charged 20% of the operating expenses. A quick calculation shows the amount to be $514.62. The second job is 34% of the total figure, and we give it 34% of the operating expenses, which is $874.87. The third, 46% of $2,573.14, is $1,183.64. In order to prove our calculations, we should add the three months back together:

$ 514.62 **Job A**
874.87 **Job B**
1,183.64 **Job C**
$2,573.13

This figure is off a mere $.01, so we can consider them accurate, and add them to our job costs.

	Job A	**Job B**	**Job C**
Job Costs	$4,215.19	$7,211.05	$ 9,811.04
Op. Exp.	514.62	874.87	1,183.64
	$4,729.81	$8,085.92	$10,994.60

In order to prove our figures, we can now add the above totals together and compare them with the total construction costs, plus the operating expenses:

Job Costs +
Operating Expenses
$ 4,729.81 **Job A**
8,085.92 **Job B**
10,994.68 **Job C**
$23,810.41

Total Costs +
Total Operating Expenses
$ 2,573.14 **total operating expenses**
21,237.28 **total costs**
$23,810.42

This proves that we have prorated our operating expenses correctly.

Any number of letters and figures can be used together to designate jobs and locations, or jobs and portions of jobs. The larger the job grows, the more breakdown might be needed, but the basic principle is the same. The guiding factor in preparing good job costs is in obtaining correct information from the people who do the work.

In the case of material, sometimes this may be purchased but not used. It will then be placed in inventory until required. In such a case, the people involved in handling it must inform the bookkeeper as to how much material is used and how much is stored. The stored material would then be placed in a "deferred material" account, and would not be costed into the jobs until it has been transferred to a specific job. When this is done, it would be on a cost-per-foot or cost-per-pound (or per-unit) basis. Labor used in handling such material would have to be added to the material cost so that it would already be included when the stored material was transferred to the job.

Time cards for employees are a must. The hours spent on the jobs should be accurate to the quarter hour. Only by having accurate material lists and time cards can the bookkeeper gain accurate costs from the sheets.

Since this is not meant to be a cost accounting course, we will stop with the basics so that you will not become too confused. If you have followed me to this point in the instructions, you have mastered the procedure of bookkeeping, and know the theory of accounting.

You have worked with the flatform ledger and progressed into the regular general ledger. You are now capable of setting up your own bookkeeping system, making the very first entry, and following through to the closing of the month, posting the general ledger, and preparation of an Income and a Financial Statement.

You have come a long, long way in these few pages. Once again, I want to offer my congratulations and best wishes.

11

The More Sophisticated Forms of Accounting *

To be successful in business, there are a few things the business person must know in order to determine where the business is going and how to control it. Up to this point, we have explored accounting in its very simplest forms in order for the neophyte to understand why certain methods are used in recording the transactions of a business. We have looked in on Inventories, Accounts Receivable, Accounts Payable, and monies due us which we are unable to collect (Bad Debts). We have learned about depreciation of equipment and fixtures and now we need to go into some of the more sophisticated forms of accounting. In operating the business, you need to have some means of knowing if you are making money and how much stock you many have on hand at any time. This is accomplished through an "Inventory Control" system.

Merchandise: Last-In-First-Out / First-In-First-Out   **LIFO/FIFO**

The types of inventory control can vary as much as do the kinds of inventory. They must be chosen to suit the kind of merchandise to be handled. The inventory of a clothing store is completely different than the inventory of a produce house, and must be handled in a different manner.

In the clothing store it would be considered a good policy to sell the oldest merchandise first in order to keep from having outdated stock on hand. But in the case of the produce house, it is a must. Produce is perishable and, if not handled properly, could spoil before being sold. With such an inventory, the business person must make certain that the oldest, or first-purchased merchandise is sold first. This is classified as a First-In-First-Out inventory, or simply FIFO. The opposite method of such handling would be Last-In-First-Out, or LIFO. This method is is often used in instances of warehousing situations which could create additional expense to move the newer merchandise in order to withdraw the older goods. This could be true of inventories such as boxed unperishable ceramic goods, furniture, plumbing supplies, and so on.

Your ability to use the LIFO inventory method for tax purposes is restricted. If you want to use the LIFO method, you must use Form 970. Read the instructions carefully to be sure you qualify to use LIFO and apply the method correctly.

*Please keep in mind that the IRS must approve a change in inventory accounting systems.

Inventory Control Value

Every business owner wants to know how much money he/she is making and how much stock is on hand at any given time. Some owners can determine this by simply looking around the store and visually estimating the value of goods still on hand. In the larger business, storing additional merchandise in warehouses requires a form of record which will give a fairly accurate value of merchandise on hand when you need it. This can be accomplished either by the "item-costing system" or by the "percentage-costing system."

Item-Costing Method

In the item-costing method (used by clothing stores, carpet contractors, furniture dealers, and some types of jewelers), the dealer will mark the cost of each item on a tag and attach it to the merchandise. This is done through a coding system which if noticed by the customer would mean nothing. For instance, we have a sofa which cost us $197 and we are supposed to sell it for $265.85. This cost would be coded on the tag with letters, such as: A=1, B=2, C=3, D=4, E=5, F=6, G=7, H=8, J=9, and K=0. Using this code, our cost figure would be posted as AJGKK. Most customers usually consider such letters as denoting either style or model numbers rather than the cost involved.

An easier coding method is to precede the cost by a digit and to succeed it by another. The same cost could be coded as 81973.

When a sale is made, the coded tag is attached to the sales slip, or the code number is written on the sales slip. The bookkeeper posts the amount of the sale on the daily sales journal, then posts the cost figures (not letters) to another column. At the end of the month, the cost column is carried over to the ledger on a "running-inventory sheet." This monthly figure is deducted from the inventory amount, leaving a figure which should equal the amount of the inventory left on hand. As new merchandise is purchased and added to stock, the cost of the incoming merchandise is added to the running inventory. The running inventory sheet is separate from the "Beginning of the Year Total" inventory sheet, and is used for monthly statements and control purposes only. The actual inventory, used in end-of-year income statements, is calculated by a physical count at the end of the year. The running inventory is adjusted to agree with the actual physical inventory.

Another use of the cost-item method of control is to post a gross profit figure in the books so the owner knows how much is being made operating the business. Again, this is for control purposes only and does not enter into the gross profit calculations at the end of the business year. The gross profit figure we use, in the case of our sofa sale, is simply the difference between the amount of the gross sale ($265.85) and the coded cost figure on the sales tag ($197), which equals $68.85. By following this procedure, the owner has a fair idea of how much gross profit has been made for the month and can see at a glance whether it would be advisable to buy that new truck or to draw enough money from the funds for a trip to Hawaii.

To determine what your net profit is for the month, or month-to-date, you need only take the gross profit figure and deduct the amount of "Operating Expenses." This figure will not be accurate, but it will be close enough to give you a control figure. And, if at the end of the year, the final profit figures are drastically different, then something is drastically wrong with the operation. You are being ripped off somewhere and should check to find out where it is happening.

Percentage Costing Method

In the "percentage" method of costing, the cost of merchandise sold is calculated by using the percentage of markup of merchandise. Drug stores, grocery stores, feed stores, and other firms which handle a large volume of small items, would find the item cost control impossible to keep up. They have controlled their inventory through using the percentage system. (New, computerized stores are using the cost-item method today, but without a computer, it would be close to impossible.)

This type of store has a set markup on most items and the non-drug or "off-beat" items sold follow such a pattern that an average percentage of over-all sales can be taken from a previous year-end Income Statement and be used as the determining factor for the following year. If the average markup of the year before was 37%, that figure will be used the following year for calculating cost of sales. This can be used in the small Mom-and-Pop grocery stores, fruit stands, notions stores, jewelry, etc. The amount of the percentage would vary with each business, but the rule of thumb for business would still hold true.

Note: In carpet sales, the cost would be figured on the cost-per-yard against the sales-price-per-yard of the material. If it is sold installed, then the cost of installation would also need to be entered into the cost-of-sales figures.

Depreciation

Changes in computing depreciation were made in the tax laws of 1981 and 1986. If you acquired the property before 1987 you use the 1981 depreciation system known as the Accelerated Cost Recovery System (ACRS). If you acquired the property after 1986, you use the new system known as the Modified Accelerated Cost Recovery System (MACRS). Both systems are covered earlier in the book. All methods for computing depreciation are ignored except for straight line, which is nothing more than dividing the number of months it is estimated an asset will exist into the cost of the asset. For information only, the following paragraphs explain another method of depreciating asset values.

Because the IRS is what it is, it is necessary to point out to them in detail that buying a truck and fixtures has cost you money. You want to deduct some of the cost from your income taxes. This is accomplished by "expensing" part of it each year under the heading of "Depreciation." The IRS will not permit you to do this in one lump sum. In many cases, it is beneficial to you not to do this. Most new businesses are not expected to make money for at least three years, and it wouldn't make sense to deduct the cost of expensive equipment and fixtures in a year you don't make a profit. It is better to spread it over a number of years by depreciation.

Sum-of-the-Digits Method

We will assume you have purchased a large van to be used in making pickups and deliveries of merchandise and desire to depreciate by the Sum-of-the-Digits method. The expected life of the truck would be seven years, so we make a work sheet showing the seven years numbered in this manner:

1
2
3
4   Add up the numbers and arrive at a total
5   of 28 units.
6
7
___
28

Now, assuming the amount of truck cost to be depreciated is $12,000, we will divide the cost by the sum of the digits (28), obtaining an answer of $428.57. This is the amount of one unit.

Starting at the top of our chart, we will depreciate the truck one unit the first year, or $428.57. The second year, we would use two units, or $857.14. The third year, three units would be used, and so on throughout the seven years of truck depreciation. By the end of that time, we will have depreciated the entire $12,000 of write-off value. The following calculations show you how this works:

1 unit	$ 428.57
2 units	857.14
3 units	1,285.71
4 units	1,714.28
5 units	2,142.85
6 units	2,571.42
7 units	2,999.99
total units	$11,999.96

The depreciation for the seven years comes to a total of $11,999.96, or only four cents less than the $12,000. That amount can be added to the last year.

Because the *Least* depreciation is taken when the truck is new, and the *Most* when the truck is on the verge of obsolescence, you find it more beneficial to take the most units at a time when it costs more to keep the truck running. It is up to you to decide which method will do you the most good.

At this point, I will explain again that payments to a bank or loan company for the truck purchase are not "expenses" to take the place of depreciation. Payments are on the *loan* which made the purchase possible for you. Payments on that loan are debited to your "Loans Payable" or "Notes Payable" account.

Accrued Expenses

Changing over from a "Cash Method" of accounting to an "Accrual Method" of accounting brings into use another set of records which we have not used up to this point. This is the Invoice Register. The Invoice Register sheet (obtainable from your office supply store) is set up similar to the check register with a date column, total amount column, a column for the name of the vendor, and various columns to post the amounts of the purchase. The columns have headings taken from the Chart of Accounts to guide us in posting the invoice amounts. Such headings are usually the merchandise-purchased accounts, and are broken down in the manner they are carried on the income statement (apparel, shoes, cosmetics, leather goods, etc.)

The amount of the invoice is posted twice; once in the total amount column, then again in the merchandise purchased column. This could be the total amount of that invoice, or broken down as shown above if those items were listed on the same invoice.

When the invoice page has been posted and totalled for the month, then the totals of the columns are posted to the general ledger to the "Expense or Merchandise Purchased" sheet in the liability section of the ledger.

Bad Debts

Operating a small business has many pitfalls, but the one capable of creating the most problems is "Credit Sales." In this day of credit cards, this type of business is not as necessary as in the past. But it does exist. In accepting credit sales, the owner accumulates a large amount of Accounts Receivable, which are funds sorely needed in order to carry on the business. Even in the best of stores, and after the best of screening of credit applicants, many charge accounts turn sour and must be considered "bad debts."

To be classified as a bad debt, the account must have had repeated attempts of collection, without results. This could cover a number of years. After the account has been classified as a bad debt and charged to the "Reserve for Bad Debts," you may post the amount of that particular account to the reserve for bad debts. This is a credit item in the asset section of the financial statement.

The following is a crude example:

Cash on Hand—Bank of America	$3,215.85	
Cash on Hand—Cash funds	40.00	
		$3,255.85
Accounts Receivable	$4,215.48	
Reserve for Bad Debts	37.20	
		$4,178.28

Assuming that the Accounts Receivable is $4,215.48 and the amount of our bad debt is $37.20, we deduct the bad debt from the amount of receivables and the balance is carried as the total receivables on the financial statement.

That same amount ($37.20) would also be posted (debited) to the bad debts expense account in the Operating Expenses section of the income statement. Anytime a bad debt is collected, it is carried as "Other Income," which is also posted to the bad debts expense account in the Operating Expenses section of the income statement. Anytime a bad debt is collected, it is carried as "Other Income," which is posted to the operating expenses section as a credit figure (negative figure which is bracketed). You have already paid taxes on the original sale and to bring in the collections as income in the sales section would be to have money which has already been taxed, taxed again. The amount of the bad debt is then deducted out of the "Reserve for Bad Debts" and "Accounts Payable." This is accomplished through a general journal entry.

Deferred Income

Deferred income is an amount of money that has been held back for some authorized purpose and will be paid at some later time. This type of income will be little used in the small business, but should be explained here.

Many times, people who receive a large grant, bonus, award, or other amount of money, will prefer that it be paid over a period of time in order to have a steady income and at the same time have less income tax liability on the amount.

If the business requires that the customer pay in advance for services or goods to be received over two or more years, deferred income becomes a real question to be discussed with your accountant or tax advisor.

This occurs particularly in the area of newsletter and magazine publishing, for example. If the customer pays for a three-year subscription to a publication, recording this income is somewhat different. If the owner were to record the full payment as income in the year received, he/she would produce an income statement which reflected an inflated and unreal picture of the profit. Excess taxes would be paid. Deferred income allows the sale (income) to be reflected over the three years (or whatever) period the expense or goods are to be rendered.

Stock Dividends

In the corporation entity (which will be explained in another chapter), the corporation is formed by the principle (or owner). The corporation produces stock which can be sold for funds to help purchase merchandise for sale, or equipment to be used in the production of merchandise to be sold. The person who buys a share of stock pays an amount set by the corporation, and holds the stock as long as he/she desires to do so. Over a period of years as the corporation grows, it will have profits in sufficient amounts that a dividend will be declared and a set amount will be paid to the stock owners as dividends. The amount of dividend each stockholder receives depends on the number of shares and the kind of stock held.

There are two kinds of stock usually placed on the market: Preferred and Common.

Preferred stock is sometimes called "Blue Chip" stock and is purchased for income rather than growth. It must receive a divident. Common stock is less expensive to buy and might not always receive a dividend. Even without dividend-payment income, the owner of Common stock will make money through the growth of the corporation, and the increase of value of his/her Common shares. The value of stock depends on the growth of the company and the demand for it on the stock market. All shares of stock carry a right to vote in corporation management elections, and to set policy trends. The amount of dividends declared on a share of stock depends on the amount of profit earned and the amount the company decides it can afford to pay out while retaining enough of the surplus for contingencies and to create additional growth.

If the business owner is incorporated and operating a profitable business, he/she should discuss with the accountant when and if a dividend should be declared. Even if all the stock is held by the owner, this is important. It can be very important for tax purposes to address this issue in order to minimize taxes and protect the corporation as an entity.

Analyzing Your Income Statement

Analyzing your Income Statement is a relatively simple operation with the help of our modern electronic calculators. It can be accomplished by anyone by following a few simple steps. Large businesses do it as part of their financial statement preparation in order to determine their business trends. In a small business, it can be equally as important.

For the sake of an illustration, let's assume that Hazel's Gift shop has prepared an income statement. She wants to analyze it in order to compare it with operations of other gift shops. Her income statement appears below.

Hazel's Gift and Novelty shop
921 Hazelwood Drive
Santa Cruz, CA 95060

Income Statement—Janaury 31, 19____

Gross Sales	$24,267.98	100.00%
Cost of Sales	14,509.23	59.79
Gross Profit	$ 9,758.75	40.21%
Operating Expenses		
Controllable Expenses		
Outside Labor	$ 29.12	.12%
Operating Supplies	492.62	2.03
Gross Wages	2,375.74	9.79
Repairs and Maintenance	116.48	.48

Advertising	388.27	1.60
Car Expense	223.26	.92
Bad Debt Expense	4.85	.02
Administrative and Legal	152.88	.63
Miscellaneous Expense	133.47	.55
Total Controllable Expenses	$3,916.69	16.14%
Fixed Expenses		
Rent Expense	$1,358.95	5.60%
Utilities	390.70	1.61
Insurance	245.10	1.01
Interest Expense	38.83	.16
Depreciation Expense	364.00	1.50
Total Fixed Expenses	$2,572.30	10.60%
Total Operating Expenses	$6,488.99	26.74%
Net Profit From Operations	$3,268.76	13.47%

Beginning at the top of the statement, place the "Cost of Sales" figure in the calculator and divide it by the "Gross Sales" figure. This is $14,509.23 divided by $24,267.98. Our answer is 59.79%. Now do the same with the "Gross Profit" figure. This is $9,758.75 divided by $24,267.98. The answer is 40.21%. Proceed down the statement, calculating each percentage figure and marking it beside the figure on your income statement. When you have finished, the sheet should look like the illustration I have provided. What we now have is an outline of where cash flow is going and by what percentage of the Gross Income.

A new business is going to have larger percentages in some items than might another store in the same business. But the longer a store is in operation, the more efficient that business should become. However, your own figures can give you some idea of how you stand in the scheme of things if you can compare them with other percentages of businesses in your field. It will also aid your own performance from one period of time to the next.

As a business evolves, it usually becomes beneficial to prepare income statements on a periodic basis, be that monthly, quarterly, or annually. This is especially true if the business is expanding or changing rapidly. By comparing your expenses and profit as a percentage of sales, you can see where your expenses are increasing and/or decreasing as a percentage, and take appropriate action where necessary.

For instance, if the business reflects a loss of 5% where it showed a profit of 10% in an earlier period, you will want to look closely at the expenses and cost of sales. This will help determine why this is happening, and allow you to take steps to cut expenses in that area, if possible. If you are experiencing increasing profit, you may want to increase salaries or invest more in advertising rather than pay heavy taxes on the profit. But, by all means, be sure to analyze the results of all the effort put into preparing this data. That is the best way you can use it to benefit and justify the expense of keeping all the records.

There are a number of publications available for the business person to use in comparing his/her averages with others in the same gross sales bracket. The Government Printing Office in Washington, D.C. has publications for the small business operator. Another is published by the National Cash Register Company. It is called "Expenses in Retail Business" and can be obtained by writing to their Marketing, Education, and Publications offices in Dayton, Ohio, 45409. This booklet contains valuable information on markup, operating ratios, and other accounting procedures which can be of benefit to the business. Much of this information is beyond the scope of this book.

12

Business Entities and What They Mean to You

One of the pleasures of owning your own business is the fact that you are your own boss, can keep your own hours, and make your own decisions. If the hours are right, and you make the right decisions, then "the sky's the limit." You could grow into a multi-million-dollar business.

As sole owner of the operation, doing business is rather simple. The bookkeeping is minimal, and as long as the business remains small, it is usually carried on under the name of the owner, such as Hansen's Shoe Shop, Quigley's Grocery, Hazel Hayworth's Apparel Store, etc. As the business grows, the owner might move into larger quarters and want to change the name to "The Eastside Supermaket," Lady Fashions Apparel," "The Shoe and Boot Hospital," etc.

Changing the name to something other than that of the owner is classified as doing business under a fictitious name, or "D/B/A" ("Doing Business As"). This is made legal by requesting a form from the County Clerk's Office, filling it out, and following the procedures in having it published in the local newspaper under the proper classification. The fictitious name then becomes the name of the store or business and remains with it as long as the owner desires. The store, if sold, often keeps the same name unless the new owners wish to change it.

The Sole Proprietorship

The Sole Proprietorship is a convenient form of ownership. But by being the sole owner, you not only make all of the decisions, but also bear the burden of all the possible mistakes. As sole owner of the business, everything you own becomes a part of that business to the extent that your car, your home, and any other property you might own, is collateral for whatever losses the store or business might have. In obtaining a loan from a lending institution, the officers of that institution may request a Financial Statement and a Statement of Net Worth, which will include the value of all properties owned by you. In the event of bankruptcy, the forms are filed for you and *all* of your property, and not for the business alone.

In the event that you have additional money to put into the business, that additional money is not a loan. It is simply an increase in your Capital Investment, and can be withdrawn at any time you desire if the profits warrant such a withdrawal.

In the Sole Proprietorship, you take all the risks, reap all the rewards, and remain an island unto yourself in the stream of business.

Partnership

A **partnership** can be composed of any number of people, from the two usually thought of as being a partnership, to whatever number might be found in an active cooperative business venture or co-op. Regardless of the number of people involved, it is still a partnership except in the corporate structure, which we will look at later.

A business owner can have multiple partners, or only one, with none of them entering into the business as active participants. Usually such a relationship is called a "silent" partnership, and is formed solely to obtain additional capital to operate the business. The silent partner(s) does not work in the business, makes no decisions, and is entitled to a share of the net profit in accordance with the money he/she put into the venture. The partner could have purchased a quarter, a third, or a half of the business, and would share in the profit accordingly.

In the open partnership, the owner could have one or more people working with him who have put money into the business for equal shares of the profits. For the sake of an illustration, we will assume two people (the owner and the partner) are sharing in the business. This will create an equal ownership of two people, and the bookkeeping is set up to give each a drawing account and a capital account to keep track of the money they put into the business and the funds they draw out.

Each partner would receive reimbursement for monies spent in the course of doing business—auto expense, travel expense, etc. Each partner might also have portions of his home expenses paid by the business because some of them might be incurred in business activities. Portions of the phone bill (such as long-distance calls, home-office deductions, etc.) would be reimbursed.

Each partner could hold insurance policies on the other in order to be compensated in case one should die. This insures against a transition period which must be endured before normal business could be resumed. This insurance expense would be a legitimate expense of the business, and would be entered into the operating expenses in the books.

In a partnership, the cash method of accounting could be used, but it would be inefficient. A double entry accrual accounting system would give more realistic values in the Financial Statement and Income Statement. After all, this is what we are looking for.

In the open partnership, each party's entire assets would become part of the business in the same manner as in the sole proprietorship. In the event of bad times or bankruptcy, both parties' assets would be forfeited to the amount of the liability. True, each partner would have a shoulder to cry on, but that is little comfort during the loss of a home and property.

In the event that one partner chooses to lead a lifestyle beyond his/her means and wants to out-do all of the big spenders, the money he/she draws from the business comes out of the net profits. If drawn to excess, it would then become a capital drawing account. In such a case, an unstable partner can bankrupt a perfectly sound business by over-indulging his/her own fantasies and whims. This means that a partner should be accepted into the business only after a great deal of considera-tion as to character and reputation.

Corporation

These are primary reasons for you to consider incorporation. Without the corporate structure of business as we know it today, this country, and most of the civilized world, would be less civilized and without the standards of living we now enjoy. The corporation has given us mass transportation, mass farming, mass industrial production of such items as automobiles, airplanes, refrigerators, television, tele-phones, and many other "modern" conveniences. Without the corporate structure, business would have been unable to amass the capital neces-sary to build the giant facilities which produce the goods of our modern world.

What can the corporate structure do for you? Very much!

A corporation is not an inanimate "it" in the sense of business. It is a being, an entity, a creation which charts its own course and is spoken of as if it were a living human being.

There are a few types of corporations. When you consider incorpor-ating, you must decide which type you desire to be. The closed, or "close," corporation (both terms are acceptable) is one which has a close-knit ownership with the stock being owned only by the principles involved. The open corporation has a number of owners through the medium of shares of stock, which has been sold in order to raise money to start the business.

In either kind of corporation, the inventory, equipment, buildings, fixtures, are all owned by the corporation. It then carries on the business as a sole proprietorship might do by hiring employees, producing goods and services, displaying goods for sale, depending on the commercial endeavor in which it is involved.

The corporation is run by a Board of Directors composed of the principles of the corporation and sometimes invited participants from other businesses. This type of makeup of the board gives the business an expertise that it might not otherwise have found in the world of business.

The directors formulate the policy of the corporation which is then handed down to the president and other officers of the company to execute.

In most states, three people are required in order to form a corporation, filling the offices of President, Vice-President, and Secre-tary/Treasurer. These officers are usually also members of the board so that they know at all times what the policy of the company is to be. The president of the corporation is the top executive officer, and it is her/his will that is followed by the officers and other employees of the corporation. In the corporate structure of big business, the board members and all principal officers may be (and are) very wealthy people. *But none of their wealth is jeopardized* by the state of the business health of the corporation. If the corporation were to fall on bad times or venture into bankruptcy (as is happening in some of our large auto manufacturers) through bad judgements and loss of large amounts of money, *none of the assets of the board members, the principal officers, or the employees* will be jeopardized by such a decline.

In Delaware, and possibly one other state, a corporation can be formed with only one person, and with little or no capital. This makes the corporate structure available for many small businesses which would be restricted from incorporating elsewhere. (A publication is now available from Enterprise Publishing, Inc., entitled: *How To Form Your Own Corporation Without a Lawyer For Under $50.* Contact them at 725 Market Street, Wilmington, Delaware 19801.)

During the growth of the small corporation, if one of the principal officers (or owners) wishes to loan money to the business, it would be handled on the books as an outside loan in the same manner as if obtained from a lending institution. In the event that the company should fail, that loan would be one of the corporate liabilities, and would receive the same consideration as any of the other creditors.

Note: In the event of a corporation obtaining a loan from a lending institution, the firm might request the signature of a "responsible party" on the contract in order to make certain there would be an opportunity to collect the unpaid balance.

Accounting for such a venture can be a very simple operation when the business is small. It can become very sophisticated as the business grows. The accounting department for a company such as General Motors or Lockheed Aircraft has a chart of accounts as long as your arm. Each department must have its own entries and each branch must have its own department entries.

When the small business decides to incorporate, it *must* have a double entry/accrual accounting system which may or may not include subsidiary ledgers for various parts of the operation. These include Accounts Receivable, Accounts Payable, Loans Payable, Loans Receivable, Employee Advances, Employee Compensation Records, etc.

By the time this happens, the owner may be too busy with the administration of the business to have the time to do the bookkeeping. He/she may have a full-time accountant or bookkeeper doing the work. But because the owner has learned the rudiments of the profession, he/she can read a Financial Statement, understand an Income Statement, and know exactly where the business is going.

It pleases me to feel that I had some small part in it.

Despite the nontax advantages of a corporation, there could be tax disadvantages. That's because the maximum corporate tax rate is 34 percent, while your individual tax rate might be only 28 percent. That means it costs six percent more to have the money earned by the corporation than by you. If you take the money out of the corporation through dividends or some other nondeductible form, the money will be taxed again when you receive it.

To avoid this situation, you can form a corporation for the nontax advantages, then make a subchapter S election for tax purposes. The S election means that the corporation will not be taxed. Instead, the income of the corporation will be taxed to the shareholders, much like the partners of a partnership are treated. This ensures that the business's income will be taxed at your top rate instead of the top corporate rate of 34%. By making the S election, however, you might lose some fringe benefits. S corporation shareholders owning two percent or more of the corporation do not get the same tax-free benefits that shareholder-employees of regular corporations get. So you probably do not want to make the S election until your corporation's taxable income is well into the top tax bracket. Then the tax savings will make up for the lost fringe benefits.

All officers of a corporation are employees of that corporation. They receive regular paychecks for the work or service they render. Even if the corporation finds it necessary to obtain a loan to pay salaries and wages, the employees must be paid.

Something to Think About

Appendix

How to tell if your business needs help.

The health of a business is determined by the guidance given it by the owner. To do so, the owner must have the necessary knowledge provided by well-kept business records.

The large, sophisticated business uses more complex methods in determining the status of the business' health. These methods include "Inventory Turnover Ratios," (which is the Net Gross Sales divided by the Balance Sheet Inventory, showing the number of times the inventory was sold and replaced during the year) and other monitoring techniques. These other techniques would include "Current Debt to Tangible Net Worth" (the difference between the owner's capital and net worth and the current liabilities that must be paid during the working year). If the Net Worth Account is less than the Current Debts, the business is in trouble.

These ratios give the administration officers of the business the information they need to make decisions in operating the business.

The small business doesn't need methods quite so elaborate.

Small businesses can, and do, become ill. They sometimes run a fever which can be detected by the owner through observing the following:

*Lack of adequate funds in the the bank.

The Accounts Payable are becoming larger and larger, but the business is still making good sales. This means the money is being used for something other than paying the invoices as they come due. If the owner is following a flamboyant and expensive lifestyle, the business will be shortlived because the money he has invested will soon be gone. The business will be forced into bankruptcy.

A simple guide for the business is the Income Statement Analysis, which was explained in Chapter 11. In making such an analysis, the owner divides each item (The Cost of Sales, The Gross Profit, The Net Profit, The Operating Expenses, Operating Accounts, and the Net Profit) by the Net Gross Sales, which gives the percentage of the money taken in which has been spent on that item or group of items. By comparing these percentage ratios with like ratios of other businesses of the same field (NCR has a book of these, and the Government Printing Office has others), the owner will know what items are using the most funds out of the cash flow. Adjustments can then be made to compensate. It might be necessary to get rid of a department or change a manner of selling in order to bring the business back to good health.

Some of the things to look for include:

1. **Payables become too large.** (The business could have a fever.)

2. **Making good sales, but never enough money to pay the bills** (Could be over-expanding, without the capital necessary for the additional business.)

3. **Equipment is sitting idle.** (Idle equipment is unnecessary equipment. Best to sell it and use the money for other things.)

4. **Owner is overdrawing Net Profits.** (Is actually withdrawing his/her capital, and since most of the money is tied up in inventory and equipment, the business will soon need a major transfusion to survive.)

5. **Employees have too much free time.** (Has too much help and the burden will drain a small business.)

6. **Doesn't have money to remit Quarterly Withholding Taxes.** (Answer could be same as #4. If not, an analysis of the Income Statement will give a clue to the problem.)

Probably the most important thing you can do for your business' health is to give it regular checkups. Above all, make sure you understand the bookkeeping and accounting functions so that the figures mean something to you. Stay on top of how your accounting books are shaping up, and you will be well informed of any areas needing attention and corrective action well before the day when it is too late to do anything about a problem.

State Tax Departments

ALABAMA
Dept. of Revenue, Inc. Tax Div.
Folsom Administration Bldg., #106
Montgomery, AL 36130
(205) 261-3355 or (205) 261-3356

ALASKA
Department of Revenue
Public Services Division
1111 W. 8th St., Room 108
Juneau, AK 99801
(907) 465-2392

ARIZONA
Department of Revenue
Forms Unit, 1700 W. Washington
Phoenix, AZ 85007
(602) 225-4260

ARKANSAS
Forms Desk
Arkansas Income Tax Section
P.O. Box 3628
Little Rock, AR 72203
(501) 682-7255

CALIFORNIA
State of California
Franchise Tax Board/Forms Request
Sacramento, CA 95840
(916) 355-0370

COLORADO
Department of Revenue
State Capitol Annex
1375 Sherman Street
Denver, CO 80261
(303) 866-5567

CONNECTICUT
State Dept. of Revenue Services
92 Farmington Avenue
Hartford, CT 06105
(203) 566-8168

DELAWARE
Division of Revenue
State Office Building
9th & French Streets
Wilmington, DE 19899
(302) 571-3300

DISTRICT OF COLUMBIA
Government of District of Columbia
Dept. of Finance & Revenue
300 Indiana Ave., N.W. Room 1046
Washington, D.C. 20001
(202) 727-6170

FLORIDA
Department of Revenue
Carlton Building
Tallahassee, FL 32301
(904) 488-6800 or (800) 872-9909

GEORGIA
Income Tax Unit, Dept. of Revenue
Trinity-Washington Building
Atlanta, GA 30334
(404) 656-4293

HAWAII
Taxpayer Service Branch
State of Hawaii, Dept. of Taxation
P.O. Box 259
Honolulu, HI 96809
(808) 548-7572

IDAHO
State Tax Commission
P.O. Box 36
Boise, ID 83722
(208) 334-7789

ILLINOIS
Department of Revenue
Box 19010
Springfield, IL 62794
(217) 782-3336
In IL (800) 732-8866

INDIANA
Department of Revenue
State Office Bldg., Room 113
100 N. Senate Avenue
Indianapolis, IN 46204
(317) 232-2216

IOWA
Iowa Department of Revenue
Hoover State Office Bldg.
Services Section
Des Moines, IA 50319
(515) 281-5370

KANSAS
Kansas Dept. of Revenue
Income Tax & Inheritance Tax Bureau
Box 12001
Topeka, KS 66612
(913) 296-3051

KENTUCKY
Revenue Cabinet
Property-Mail Services
Frankfort, KY 40620
(502) 564-3658

LOUISIANA
State Dept. of Rev. & Taxation
P.O. Box 201
Baton Rouge, LA 70821
(504) 925-7532

MAINE
Bureau of Taxation
Income Tax Section
State Office Bldg.
Augusta, ME 04333
(207) 289-3695

MARYLAND
Comptroller of the Treasury
Income Tax Division
State Income Tax Building
Annapolis, MD 21411
(301) 974-3453

MASSACHUSETTS
Department of Revenue
100 Cambridge Street
Boston, MA 02204
(617) 727-4392

MICHIGAN
Revenue Admin. Services Division
Treasury Building
Lansing, MI 48922
(517) 373-2873

MINNESOTA
Minnesota Dept. of Revenue
Forms Distribution Center
Form B-20
St. Paul, MN 55145
(612) 296-9118

MISSISSIPPI
State Tax Commission
Jackson MS 39205

MISSOURI
Director of Revenue
Jefferson City, MO 65107

MONTANA
Department of Revenue
Helena, MT 59620

NEBRASKA
State Tax Commission
State Capitol
Lincoln, NE 68509

NEVADA
State Tax Commission
Carson City, NV 89710

NEW HAMPSHIRE
State Tax Commission
Concord, NH 03301

NEW JERSEY
Treasury Department
Division of Taxation
Trenton, NJ 08625

NEW MEXICO
Bureau of Revenue
Santa Fe, NM 87503

NEW YORK CITY
Finance Administration
Dept. of Tax Collection
P.O. Box 446, Canal St. Station
New York, NY 10013
(212) 966-3025

NORTH CAROLINA
Department of Revenue
P.O. Box 25000
Raleigh, NC 27640
(919) 733-3261

NORTH DAKOTA
Tax Commissioner
State Capitol
Bismarck, ND 58505
(701) 224-2770

OHIO
Ohio Dept. of Taxation
P.O. Box 2476
Columbus, OH 43216
(614) 466-6712

OKLAHOMA
Tax Commission
2501 Lincoln Blvd.
Oklahoma City, OK 73194
(405) 521-3108

OREGON
Oregon Dept. of Revenue
955 Center Street, N.E.
Salem, OR 97310

PENNSYLVANIA
Dept. of Revenue
Tax Forms Services Unit
2850 Turnpike Industrial Dr.
Middletown, PA 17057

RHODE ISLAND
Dept. of Administration
Div. of Taxation
289 Promenade Street
Providence, RI 02903
(401) 277-3934

SOUTH CAROLINA
South Carolina Tax Commission
P.O. Box 125
Columbus, SC 29214
(803) 758-3751

SOUTH DAKOTA
Department of Revenue
700 Governor's Drive
Pierre, SD 57501
(605) 773-3311

TENNESSEE
Tennessee Dept. of Revenue
504 Andrew Jackson State
  Office Building
Nashville, TN 37242
(615) 741-2481

TEXAS
Comptroller of Public Accounts
State of Texas
111 East 17th
Austin, TX 78774
(512) 463-4600

UTAH
State Tax Commission
Heber M. Wells Building
160 East 300 South
Salt Lake City, UT 84134
(801) 530-4847

VERMONT
Vermont Department of Taxes
109 State Street
Montpelier, VT 05602
(802) 828-2515

VIRGINIA
Department of Taxation
Commonwealth of Virginia
P.O. Box 1317
Richmond, VA 23210
(804) 257-8205 or (804) 257-8055

WASHINGTON
Department of Revenue
General Administration Bldg.
AX-02
Olympia, WA 98504
(206) 753-5540

WEST VIRGINIA
State Tax Department,
Income Tax Division
P.O. Drawer 1071
Charleston, WV 25324
(304) 344-2068

WISCONSIN
Wisconsin Dept. of Revenue
Attn: Shipping & Mailing Section
P.O. Box 8903
Madison, WI 53703
(608) 266-1961

WYOMING
Secretary of State
Capitol Building
Cheyenne, WY 82002
(307) 777-7311

INTERNAL REVENUE SERVICE
Check local blue or white pages for local office under "United States Government-
Internal Revenue Service." For forms and publications only call 1-800-424-FORM.

Index

A

Accelerated Cost Recovery System, 41
accounting, different types, 1
accounting/bookkeeping, difference, 24
accounts payable, 20, 150
accounts receivable, 36, 37, 47, 139
accrual accounting, 1-3, 5, 8
accumulated totals, 13
advertising agencies, 41
advertising expense, 25, 39, 45
architects, 41
assets, 19, 21, 117
auditors, 98
automobile expense, 108

B

bad debts, 46, 139
balance sheet, 23, 58, 59, 60
bank statement, 63-65
beauty parlors, 41
bookkeeping/accounting, difference, 24
brackets, use of, 29, 47

C

capital, 21, 22
cash and carry businesses, 1, 33
cash and sales journal, 32, 47
cash basis accounting, 1, 3, 5, 15

cash drawer, 6
cash in bank, 19
cash investment, 21
cash register, 1, 29, 39
cash sales, 2, 27, 48
charge sales 2, 31, 33, 36
charge slips, 36
chart of accounts, 45
checking account, 39
check distribution sheet, 39, 47, 51, 80
checks/checkbooks, 22, 79
clothing deduction, 112
contractor, accounting for, 127
corporation, 18, 147-148
cost of merchandise sold, 2, 54
cost of sales, 3, 14, 58, 117
credit figures, 47
credits, 25, 26

D

debits, 25, 26
debts, bad, 46, 139
deductions, 112
deferred income, 141
dentists, 41, 112
deposits, 27, 74, 83
depreciation, 40, 41, 112, 137
depreciation expense, 41, 137
doctors, 41, 112
double entry cash method, 25-32